Russia and the USSR 1900–95

Richard Radway

Stanley Thornes (Publishers) Ltd

Designed and typeset by Hilary Norman
Illustrations by Hardlines and Beverly Curl (pages 12–13)
Picture research by Julia Hanson

Original line illustrations © Stanley Thornes (Publishers) Ltd
1996

First published in 1996 by:
Stanley Thornes (Publishers) Ltd
Ellenborough House
Wellington Street
CHELTENHAM GL50 1YW
England

96 97 98 99 00 / 10 9 8 7 6 5 4 3 2 1

A catalogue record for this book is available from the British
Library.

ISBN 0–7487–2547–4

Cover photograph: Rex Features

Printed and bound in Hong Kong

Acknowledgements

b = bottom, t top, l left, r right, c centre

AKG, London 48, 50, 51t & bl, 52t;
Bodleian Library Oxford (1784. c.63) 21t;
Bridgeman Art Library 51br;
The British Museum 38t, 64b;
Bundesarchiv, Koblenz 811;
Culver Pictures 15t;
Hulton-Deutsch Collection 25t, 35, 40, 44, 571,
    83c, 87r;
David King Collection 5t, 6t, 9cr, 12t, 14, 15b, 16,
    17t, 18, 19, 23b, 25b, 26tl & br, 26-7, 27c, 28,
    29c, 30t, 32t, 32b, 33, 36t & b, 38b, 39t & b, 41t
    & b, 42, 45, 46, 49t & b, 52b, 53t, c & b, 55t & b,
    56t & b, 57r, 58, 59l & r, 61bl, 62, 63, 64t, 65, 66,
    68, 70tl, tr & b, 71, 72t & b, 73, 74, 76b, 77t, c &
    b, 78t, 82, 83, 84t;
John Frost Historical Newspapers/MSI 85t;
Alexander Chunosov/Network 69;
Novosti 8tr, 27br;
AFP/PA News 95b;
Range Pictures 27tr, 86;
Rex Features Front Cover, 4b, 871, 89b, 90, 93, 94;
Roger-Viollet 57c;
SCRSS 23t;
Societe de Geographie Francaise, Paris 8c;
Centre for the Study of Cartoons and Caricature,
    University of Kent, Canterbury/Solo Syndication 7;
Gamma/Frank Spooner Pictures 4t;
Victoria and Albert Museum 8br;
Visual Arts Library 61br.

71b and 78b, From *Stalin* by Jonathan Lewis and
Philip Whitehead, Methuen London, 1990 (Plates 5
and 6). Reproduced courtesy of the artist's estate.
Photo Albert Lekhmus.

Every effort has been made to contact copyright
holders. The publishers apologise to anyone whose
rights have been overlooked, and will be happy to
rectify any errors or omissions.

Other Key History titles for GCSE:

Key Themes of the Twentieth Century (Philip Sauvain)
Modern America (Chris Macdonald and Jon Nichol)
South Africa in the Twentieth Century
(Hamish Macdonald and Barry Williamson)

A Teacher's Guide accompanies each title.

Contents

Introduction: A century of revolution

Source A The end of communism in Russia. This photograph, taken in Moscow on 22 August 1991, shows the statue of the head of Lenin's secret police, Dzerzhinsky, being removed. It was one of many statues of Communist heroes which were destroyed after the fall of the communist government.

The beginning and the end of communism

On 19 August 1991, Boris Yeltsin stood on a tank and addressed the huge crowd in front of the Russian parliament building. 'Citizens of Russia! On the night of 18 August 1991 the lawfully elected President Gorbachev was deposed. I am calling on all soldiers: do not join the coup! We demand a general strike!' Yeltsin was the elected President of the Russian Republic. There were 200 000 people on the streets of Leningrad and another 50 000 on the streets of Moscow.

There had been similar scenes in February 1917. Then a general strike led to the fall of Tsar Nicholas II, the all-powerful ruler of Russia.

Before 1917, the Russian Empire had been the name given to the huge area which had been conquered by Russia over the previous 400 years (See Source **D**). In 1924, after the communist revolution, the communist leaders had renamed it the USSR, or Soviet Union. The republic of Russia was in control and the new Soviet Union was still often referred to as Russia.

In 1991 Soviet army tanks rolled through Moscow. The Communist Party had ruled the country for 74 years, but a group of leading communists believed that the policies of the President of the USSR, Mikhail Gorbachev, were going to end that. Gorbachev was allowing the republics which made up the Soviet Union to elect their own leaders, just as the Russian Republic had elected Yeltsin. Therefore, a group of eight leaders of the Communist Party tried to seize power and replace President Gorbachev. However, faced with such opposition, the communist leaders gave in after just 56 hours.

In the next few days the rule of the all-powerful Communist Party collapsed just as quickly as the old tsarist regime had 74 years before. The huge crowds in the streets had shown they no longer wanted to be ruled by the Communist Party.

Source B Crowds of protesters prevent tanks from entering Red Square in Moscow on 20 August 1991

Russia – problems and solutions

Yet it was not simply the manner in which these two regimes had fallen which seemed so similar. The tsar and the communist leaders had faced similar problems. They both wanted to turn Russia into a modern world power, yet they both governed an empire made up of many different races, not all of whom wanted to be ruled by Russia. Russia did not even grow enough food for its people to eat.

The solutions to these problems which the old and new regimes followed were often very similar. Both attempted to destroy opposition through the use of secret police, and both saw the development of industry as vital. For both regimes, the problems faced were those created by the nature of the Russian Empire. They are the same problems which face the current government of the Russian Republic and the other states which have emerged from the collapse of the USSR.

From communist state to superpower

Following the events of August 1991, the country which had experienced the first ever communist revolution, and which had been the model for communism around the world, was no longer a communist state. This book tells how Russia became the first communist state and how it developed from a country with a population the majority of which could neither read nor write, into one of the two superpowers of the twentieth century.

Source C   The end of the tsars in 1917. The head of a statue of Tsar Alexander III which had been destroyed. As in 1991, statues of hated former rulers were destroyed now that the people had a chance to show their feelings.

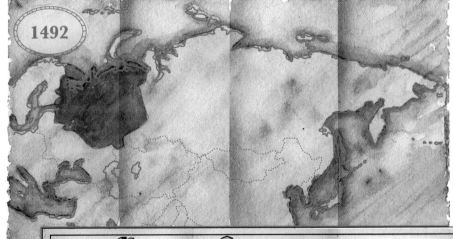

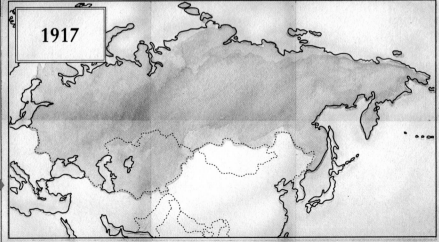

Source D
These maps show the expansion of the Russian Empire between 1462 and 1917 as it conquered more and more neighbouring territories

1492

1917

1 The Russian Empire

The Russian Empire in 1900

▶ **What problems did Russia face in 1900?**

Source A Tsar Nicholas II with his wife Alexandra and his five children

The Royal Family

sar Nicholas had married his cousin, the German princess Alexandra. Although they had five children only one of them was a boy and this was little Alexei, who is shown in the front of the photo in his sailor suit.

A boy was needed to be the heir to the throne. Unfortunately, Alexei suffered from haemophilia, an incurable disease which prevents the blood from clotting so that even a slight injury might cause the sufferer to bleed to death. Alexei would never be strong enough to rule Russia, although his parents desperately hoped that he would get better.

The power of the tsar

Russia was ruled by the tsar. He was an autocrat. That means he had complete power to make laws and govern as he wished. There was no parliament and all political parties were banned. As a result, people who opposed the tsar increasingly turned to terrorism. In 1881 a group called 'People's Will' had killed Tsar Alexander II with a bomb. After this, the secret police – the Okhrana – was created. Spies who worked for Okhrana managed to infiltrate many of the groups opposed to the tsar. More and more of the tsar's opponents were sent to prison camps in Siberia.

Those members of opposition groups who were not in prison found it safer to live in exile outside Russia. The tsar also kept the people in check by using conscription into the army as a punishment. Conscripts were forced to serve for 25 years and conditions were so harsh that during the reign of Nicholas I (1825–55) over one million men died during peacetime.

The cost of the army took up 45 per cent of the nation's budget, compared to just 4 per cent spent on education. The Russian Orthodox Church also played an important role in maintaining the power of the tsarist autocracy. For over 400 years it had been an independent Church. It taught that 'God commands us to love and obey every authority, and particularly the tsar.'

Source B Convicts in Siberia

The Empire

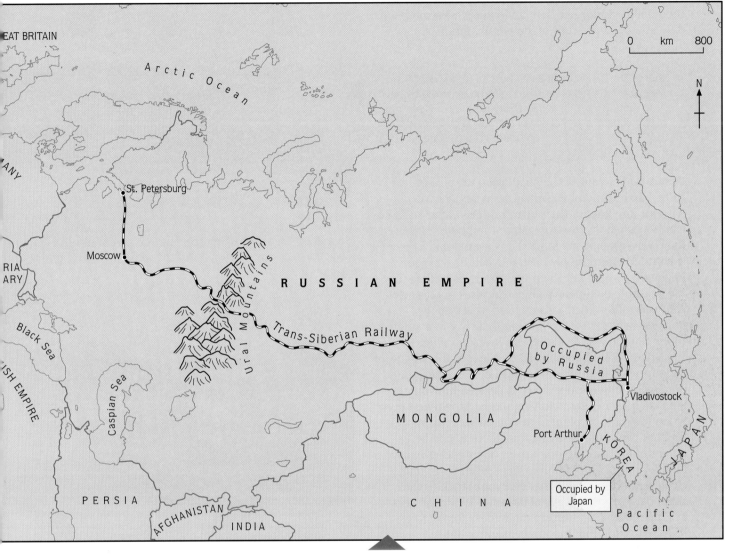

Source C A map of the Russian Empire in 1905

Russia in 1905 was an empire. Over the previous 400 years Russia had conquered a number of other neighbouring states, whose people still resented being ruled by Russia. The Russian census of 1897 revealed a total population of about 125 million, of whom approximately 55 million were Russian, with the remaining 70 million consisting of 22 different nationalities.

The Russian Empire was enormous, stretching over 6000 kilometres from St. Petersburg in the west to Vladivostok in the east. Even when the Trans-Siberian Railway was finally completed in 1917 the journey still took 13 days. However, about 70 per cent of the population lived in the area to the west of the Ural Mountains.

Questions

1 What reasons can you find on these pages to help explain why the government of the tsar was so unpopular by 1900?

2 What reasons can you find to suggest why most people in Russia obeyed the tsar's government?

Life in the countryside

About 75 per cent of the land in Russia was owned by the nobility and other rich landowners who made up only about 10 per cent of the population.

Source D   The house of a rich Russian landowner. The rich were able to live in great luxury. The house would be full of servants so that the family could live a life of ease. In this photograph, the abolition of serfdom is being read to the peasants on the estate, in 1861.

About 80 per cent of the population were peasants. Until 1861 many of them had been serfs (slaves) without any land of their own, but even after serfdom was abolished in 1861 life did not improve. Although they were given some land, the peasants had to pay for it with large annual payments (called Redemption Payments) which left them very poor. As well as this, the peasants paid nearly all of the taxes and the rich paid very little. The peasants lived in very poor housing, often with a whole family living in a single room. Source E shows a typical Russian village.

Village life was organised by the mir, the village commune. A meeting of the head of every household made all the major decisions. It decided how much land each family got, what should be grown and even when it should be planted. It offered security for Russian peasants, ensuring that there would be enough food for everyone unless bad weather caused a famine, since bigger families were given more land. However, it also meant that everyone stuck to the same old-fashioned ways of farming. While farmers in England had been using machinery for over one hundred years, the Russian peasants still used wooden ploughs and went into the fields as a family and harvested their crops with hand tools.

Source E   The village of Borispol near Kiev, in about 1880. Compare the houses in this photograph with the one in Source D.

Source G   The increase in the population of the Russian Empire 1870–1913

Source F   A meeting of a village mir

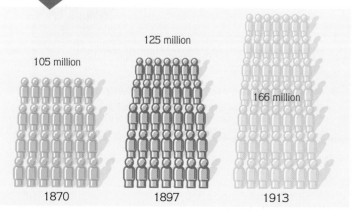

105 million

125 million

166 million

| 1870 | 1897 | 1913 |

The population of the Russian Empire was expanding rapidly. This meant there was less land for each peasant family. Large numbers of young male peasants left the countryside to try and find work in the towns.

Life in the towns and cities

By 1900 Russia had far less industry than countries like Britain and Germany. In the late nineteenth century Russia experienced a 'great spurt' in industrial production. The government feared that if Russia did not build up her industry she would no longer be a great power in the world. Between 1880 and 1906 Russian industrial production increased by over 300 per cent. This meant that there were jobs in the cities for those peasants who were leaving the countryside, and this encouraged more to follow.

As a result the population of Russian cities increased at an astonishing rate. For example, the population of St. Petersburg in 1881 was 928 000, but by 1900 this had increased to 1 439 600. The conditions the workers lived in were terrible. About 40 per cent of houses had no running water or sewage system. Working hours were long, usually around 12 hours a day, and pay was very low. Employers did not worry about the safety of their workers, and at the Putilov works in St. Petersburg there was an average of 15 accidents per month. As many of the workers were young men, the factory owners simply built dormitories for them to live in, cramming dozens in a small space. This had the unexpected result of making it much easier for the workers to organise their protests, and so strikes became common as the workers tried to improve their conditions.

The situation became even worse after 1900 when a slump in the world economy threw many industrial workers out of work and on to the streets.

However, not everyone who lived in the towns and cities was poor. As Russian industry grew, many of the factory owners and merchants became extremely rich and were able to build palaces as splendid as those of the nobles. However, most Russian merchants and factory owners were not so wealthy, but they still lived in much better conditions than the workers. These merchants and factory owners formed a class of people known as the *bourgeoisie* (see pages 12–13). The father of the writer of Source **J** was a typical Russian merchant of the time.

Source J A merchant's life

We had no servant at home, nor did we eat from gold or silver dishes. The meal was substantial but we rarely had wine. My father did buy pictures and our house contained a number of good examples of work by Russian artists.

Source H Russian coal production 1880–1913

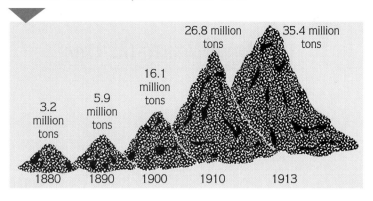

Source I A workmen's dormitory

Questions

1 **a)** In what ways did the mir make life easier for the peasants?
   b) Why do you think that the mir made it difficult to introduce modern farming methods into Russia?

2 Compare Source **D** and Source **E**. What were the differences between the living conditions of landowners and peasants?

3 Look at the information on this page. What were the results of the rapid industrialisation of Russia? Divide your answer into those results which the Russian government was *trying* to achieve and those which it was *not* trying to achieve.

4 Do you think that the people of Russia would have been pleased with the effects of industrialisation on Russia?

   To answer this question, consider each of the following groups and decide how they would have reacted to the changes you have identified in Question 3.
   a) Landowners
   b) Peasants
   c) Factory owners and merchants
   d) Factory workers.

Opposition to the tsar

Before 1905 there were many people in Russia who opposed the government of the tsar. Some of them were members of organised groups who hoped to change the way the country was governed.

Liberals
Liberals believed in freedom of speech and that the government should be elected by the people.

Zemstva
In 1864 Tsar Alexander II had introduced elected local councils which were called *zemstva*. However, the peasants had only 40 per cent of the membership, so the zemstva were dominated by landowners. Increasingly these landowners supported Liberal views, but no Liberal political parties existed until 1905 when the Octobrists and the Kadets were formed.

Octobrists
The Octobrists hoped for slow, gradual reform, to be introduced by the tsar. They were called the Octobrists because they agreed with the tsar's October Manifesto (see page 17). Their main support came from rich landowners and large industrialists.

The Kadets (KDs)
The Kadets, or Constitutional Democrats, believed in a faster pace of reform than the Octobrists. They demanded a national parliament elected by the people. This would introduce equal rights for all people and limit the power of the tsar. Their main support came from professionals such as lawyers, smaller industrialists and landowners.

Weaknesses
They received very little support from the peasants and industrial workers. Although they agreed that the conditions of the peasants and workers had to be improved, most Liberals were frightened by the violence and disorder of peasant and worker protests.

Populists
In the nineteenth century there were a number of groups who were made up mainly of young rich people. They hoped to gain the support of the peasantry to force the landowners to give up their land and divide it among the peasants. However, in general the peasants did not trust them.

'People's Will'
With the failure to gain the support of the peasants, some Populists turned to terrorism and formed a group known as 'People's Will'. Their most significant success was in 1881 when they assassinated Tsar Alexander II with a bomb.

Social Revolutionaries (SRs)
Formed in 1901 by Victor Chernov. The SRs were an alliance of various populist groups. They wanted to abolish land ownership and 'return land to those who worked it'. As a result, they were very strongly supported by peasants. The SRs also hoped to gain the support of industrial workers. Their Battle Organisation continued the terror tactics of 'People's Will'. In 1904 they assassinated the government minister Plehve, and the following year the tsar's uncle, Grand Duke Sergei. Between 1901 and 1905 they carried out 2000 assassinations.

Weaknesses
Although probably the party with the most support, the SRs were not a single party, but were made up of different groups with different aims. The moderates were willing to work for reform and they took part in the Duma, the parliament set up by the tsar in 1906. The more extreme SRs rejected the Duma and wanted a revolution.

1 Why do you think that the SRs were the most popular opposition group in Russia?

2 Why did the Mensheviks believe that all the opposition parties should work together?

3 Why did Lenin oppose the idea that all opposition parties should work together?

Questions

4 Complete the table. Which party do you think was the greatest threat to the tsar? Give your reasons.

	Kadets	SRs	Mensheviks	Bolsheviks
Strengths				
Weaknesses				

Marxists

Followers of Karl Marx and his teachings. The theories put forward by Marx are explained on the next spread.

Social Democrats (RSDLP)

The All-Russian Social Democratic Labour Party was formed in 1898 by George Plekhanov. He had already translated Marx's works into Russian and became known as 'the father of Russian Marxism'. The Social Democrats believed that the rapid industrialisation of the late nineteenth century would eventually produce an industrial working class which would revolt and bring about the socialist state that the Social Democrats wanted (see the next spread on Marxism). In 1903 the Social Democrats split into two groups – the Mensheviks and the Bolsheviks – and they later became two separate parties.

Mensheviks

The Mensheviks were led by Julius Martov. They believed that:
- The party should attract as many members as it could.
- The working class in Russia was not yet large enough to hold a successful revolution.
- The Mensheviks should work with the SRs and the Liberals so that industry could develop and a large enough working class would eventually be produced.

Bolsheviks

The Bolsheviks were led by Vladimir Ulanov, known as Lenin. Like many revolutionaries, he took a false name to help escape the attention of the tsar's secret police. The Bolsheviks believed that:
- The party should consist of a small number of committed members, who would carry out the revolution on behalf of the industrial working class (known as the 'proletariat').
- Since the party would act as the 'vanguard of the proletariat' and carry out the revolution, there was no need to wait for a bourgeois (middle class) revolution to occur first.
- There should be no co-operation with other parties. The Bolsheviks alone would lead the revolution.

Weaknesses

Most of the Bolshevik and Menshevik leaders were in foreign countries in order to escape the tsar's secret service, the Okhrana. Lenin himself was in Switzerland. Despite this, the Okhrana still managed to place its agents in senior positions in the Social Democrat Party, so that in 1914 three of the seven-man Central Committee were police agents. To make matters worse, support for the Social Democrats was divided, since the Mensheviks and the Bolsheviks increasingly treated each other as enemies rather than friends.

What is Marxism?

Karl Marx

The theory of Marxism

The Bolsheviks were Marxists, but what does this actually mean? Karl Marx was a German who believed that history progressed in a series of stages, and that every country would pass through each stage until it finally reached the perfect state of communism. What caused a country to pass from one stage to the next was a revolution carried out by the oppressed class against the ruling class. As Marx explained in the opening line of *The Communist Manifesto*, which he wrote in 1848:

'The history of all hitherto existing society is the history of class struggles.'

Marx himself compared revolution to a mole, burrowing underground for long periods, undermining the existing society and then spectacularly bringing it down when the mole emerged in the daylight.

Capitalism

The bourgeoisie, especially factory owners, now dominate. Most people become factory workers – the proletariat. Capitalism makes the bourgeoisie very rich, but the proletariat do not share this wealth. Capitalism is a system based on the belief that factories and land work more efficiently if they are owned by private individuals and not the state. The owners want to make sure that things work efficiently so that they will earn as big a profit as possible.

Feudalism

All land is owned by a few people – the aristocracy. Most people are peasants who work on the land owned by the aristocracy. Some of them prosper and a third class – the bourgeoisie – develops. They are merchants, factory owners and the like. They resent the power of the aristocracy, who make laws which help landowners but not the bourgeoisie.

Primitive society

No classes and no one owns any land. Everyone is equal.

A bourgeois revolution

The bourgeoisie eventually revolt and overthrow the landowners.

Communism
Everyone is equal. There is enough for everyone and it is distributed according to a person's needs. Government 'withers away'.

Socialism
The dictatorship of the proletariat. The workers gain control. Industry and land are taken over by the proletariat so that everyone shares in the wealth produced. Gradually people become more equal and classes disappear.

Gradual change

A proletarian revolution
The workers eventually revolt against their exploitation.

Questions

1 According to Marx, how does a revolution work?

2 Why is there no revolution to lead from socialism to communism?

3 Look back at what you read in the first unit, on the Russian Empire in 1900. Which of these stages do you think Russia had reached by the beginning of the twentieth century?

The Revolution of 1905

 **Why was there a revolution in 1905?
Why did it fail?**

Source A A Report by the French Consul in the town of Kharkov, October 1905

Work stopped everywhere; on the railways, in all factories, workshops, in shops of all types, the whole population was on the streets. People began to ransack arms stores and smash the windows of large shops. Students, directed by lawyers, doctors and teachers, set up barricades.

Source B A report by the tsar's Chief Minister, Witte, October 1905

The railways were on strike, almost all traffic in the streets had stopped, street lighting was no more, the inhabitants of St. Petersburg feared to go out on the streets at night.

Look at Sources **A** and **B**. They show that in October 1905 the tsar's government had lost control. There was a national strike involving 2.5 million people. In the first two units we saw that many Russians were discontented. The factory workers lived and worked in appalling conditions, peasants did not have enough land, while the rich had far more than they needed. Rich liberals felt that the problems of Russia could only be changed if the tsar's autocratic rule was ended and an elected parliament created. Yet these discontents had existed for many years. They were the *long-term* causes of a revolution. What was it that caused a revolution to break out in 1905 rather than any other year?

There were two events that triggered the revolution of 1905: the war against Japan and the massacre of Bloody Sunday.

War with Japan 1904–5

At the beginning of Tsar Nicholas' reign, Japan had captured Port Arthur from China (see Source **C** on page 7). However, Russia wanted this ice-free port for use by her own Pacific navy, and so forced the Japanese to hand it back to China. Then the Russians leased it from China and built a railway link from Port Arthur to the Trans-Siberian Railway. The Japanese felt humiliated, and so in 1904 they launched a surprise attack on Russia, and a war began. The Russians assumed that they would easily defeat Japan, a small country which they believed was very backward and no match for a great empire like Russia.

In fact, the war turned into a national humiliation for the Russians. When the Japanese launched their first naval attack on the Russian Pacific navy at Port Arthur, many of the Russian officers were on shore, attending a dance being given by the admiral's wife. The Russian ships even had their lights on, and so were easy targets. The Russian Baltic navy was then sent to help Port Arthur, even though this meant it had to sail half way around the world.

However, despite being well defended, Port Arthur surrendered to the Japanese in December 1904, long before the Baltic navy arrived. When the navy finally did get there in May 1905, it was sunk by the Japanese in the straits of Tsushima.

The importance of the war with Japan was that it convinced many people that change was necessary. The tsar and his ministers were leading the country to disaster.

Source C A Russian cartoon showing how easy the Russians thought it would be to defeat the Japanese navy. This shows how much the Russians underestimated the Japanese.

Bloody Sunday

Within one month of the defeat at Port Arthur, on 22 January 1905, protesters gathered in the Russian capital, St. Petersburg. They were led by a priest, Father Gapon. Their aim was to march to the Winter Palace and present a petition to the tsar. The petition explained that the people 'are approaching the terrible moment when death is better than continuing to live with these intolerable sufferings. We have no human rights, not even the right of speaking, thinking, meeting, discussing our needs'. However, the tsar was not in the Winter Palace, but the protesters did not know this. Troops in front of the Palace fired on the unarmed demonstrators.

Source D A photograph of the march in St. Petersburg on 22 January 1905

Source E Soldiers firing on protesters in the Winter Palace Square

Source F Soldiers attacking the rebels on Bloody Sunday

The events of 22 January became known as 'Bloody Sunday'. The Russian government claimed that 96 people were killed and 333 injured. It is very difficult to find out how many people were actually killed, but around 1000 is probably a more accurate estimate.

When historians try and work out what has happened in the past they have to use a range of sources, such as photographs, paintings and written accounts. Quite often these sources seem to conflict with one another. However, the job of historians is to decide how to judge these various sources and to try and work out for themselves what they think happened.

Source G By a British eyewitness

Near the Winter Palace the crowd grew and pressed on and on. Then the troops fired, bringing down little boys perched on trees in a neighbouring public garden, and killing and wounding many men and women.

Source H By Alexander Kerensky, a Russian eyewitness

Along the Nevsky Prospekt (the main road in St. Petersburg) came row upon row of orderly and solemn workers, dressed in their best clothes. Gapon, marching in front, was carrying a cross and a number of workers were holding portraits of the tsar. We heard the sound of bugles. The marchers came to a halt, uncertain as to what the bugles meant. Just then, cavalry rode out and the first volley of shots rang out. The first volley was fired in the air, but the second was aimed at the crowd and a number of people fell to the ground. The crowd began running in every direction.

The Revolution

In February 1905 the tsar's uncle, the Grand Duke Sergei, was assassinated. Strikes and riots spread across Russia. In Odessa there was a mutiny on board the battleship *Potemkin*. This was serious for the tsar because the Black Sea navy was the only one of his three navies remaining after the disastrous war against Japan. If the mutiny had spread to the army, the tsar would have had no troops to put down the revolt. In October the general strike described in Sources A and B (on page 14) began to paralyse the country.

In the capital, St. Petersburg, an organisation had been set up to co-ordinate the strikes. This was the St. Petersburg soviet. This consisted of representatives of the factory workers. The soviet became the effective government of St. Petersburg, and for the first time the workers held some sort of power in Russia.

Question

1 In what way do Sources **D** and **H** support the view that many people in Russia still wanted the tsar as their ruler?

2 Source **F** is a painting. What differences can you find between the story it tells and that shown by Source **E**?

3 Which source does support what is shown in Source **F**?

4 Photographs are more useful to the historian than written sources. Use Sources **D** and **E** and Sources **G** and **H** to help you to explain whether you agree or disagree with this statement.

Trotsky

Trotsky

Trotsky was born Leon Bronstein, but like most revolutionaries he adopted another name to try and escape detection by the tsar's secret police. Trotsky joined the RSDLP (see page 11) in 1896, and in 1903 he opposed Lenin and joined the Mensheviks. After the 1905 Revolution he escaped to Western Europe and tried to bring the two halves of the party back together. He failed, and in 1917 joined Lenin and the Bolsheviks.

The SRs, Mensheviks and Bolsheviks all realised the importance of this power, and got their members elected to the executive committee of the soviet. The chairman of the soviet was Leon Trotsky. Following the success of the St. Petersburg soviet, soviets appeared in many other cities as well. The tsar's chief minister, Witte, convinced the tsar that the only way to end the crisis was to give in to the demands of the rebels. On the third day of the strike, the tsar issued the October Manifesto, which promised freedom of speech and belief as well as a parliament. These promises won the support of the middle classes. Many of them had been very frightened by the violence of the workers and they wanted to see an end to the Revolution.

The Liberal politician Struve declared 'Thank god for the tsar, who has saved us from the people'.

In November the tsar announced the end of redemption payments in order to pacify the peasants. These were the heavy payments which the peasants had to make for the land which they received after they had been freed from serfdom. This meant that the industrial workers were isolated as the only group whose demands had not been met. Their revolts, such as a general strike in Moscow in December 1905, were crushed with great brutality by troops which had returned from the war with Japan. The Revolution was over.

The Revolution had not been an organised attempt to overthrow the tsar. Instead, it had been a series of unconnected and scattered outbursts of violence and protest amongst the industrial workers and peasants. In January 1905 most of the main revolutionary leaders, such as Lenin, were not even in the country. Also, most of the army remained loyal, so that the later riots could be crushed.

Loss of Port Arthur

Dec.	Jan.	Feb.	March	April	May	June	July	August	Sept.	Oct.	Nov.
1904						1905					

Questions

1 Draw a timeline like the one above, of events in Russia from December 1904 to November 1905. Mark the following events on your timeline:
   a) The loss of Port Arthur (this is done for you)
   b) Bloody Sunday
   c) Assassination of Grand Duke Sergei
   d) Defeat by Japanese at Tsushima
   e) *Potemkin* Mutiny
   f) October general strike
   g) October Manifesto
   h) Ending of redemption payments
   i) Defeat of Moscow strike

2 a) Make a list of as many causes as you can for the 1905 Revolution.
   b) Which are *long-term* causes?
   c) Which are *short-term* causes?

3 Look at the following list of reasons for the failure of the 1905 Revolution. See if you can think of any more, and add them to the list. Draw a table with two columns, one headed '**Strengths of tsarism**' and one headed '**Weaknesses of the opposition**'. Now sort the following reasons into one or other of the two columns.
   a) Liberals bought off by October Manifesto
   b) Loyalty of most troops
   c) Strikes and riots not co-ordinated
   d) Middle classes fear violence of the workers
   e) Revolts were a protest, not an attempt to overthrow the tsar

4 Look at your completed table. Explain whether you feel it is true to say that the failure of the 1905 Revolution was due to the strength of the tsarist government.

A reform of tsarism?

 Did the tsar cure the problems which had caused the 1905 Revolution?

Repression

The tsar had survived the 1905 Revolution. He appointed a new chief minister, Peter Stolypin, and he sought to punish those who had been responsible in order to teach the Russian people a lesson. In 1906 over 1000 people were executed for their part in the revolution and a further 21 000 were sent to prison camps in Siberia. Between 1907 and 1911 a further 1800 were hanged, and the noose became known as 'Stolypin's necktie'. However, Stolypin believed that such repressive measures needed to be backed up with positive changes to prevent another revolution breaking out in the future.

Political reforms

In the October Manifesto the tsar had won the support of many liberals with his promise of an elected parliament or Duma. Therefore elections were held and in 1906 the Duma met for the first time. Yet, as Source **A** shows, the tsar was not willing to allow the Duma to have any real power.

Source A The Fundamental Laws of 1906

The tsar possesses the initiative in all legislative matters. No law can come into force without his approval.

In other words, the Duma could only consider laws which the tsar suggested, and he could then veto any of their decisions – that is, he could reject anything that the Duma had decided.

Source B Nicholas II in 1908

I have created the Duma not to instruct me but to advise me.

Given his attitude in Source **B** it is hardly surprising that Nicholas quickly ended the Dumas of 1906 and 1907. However, the tsar needed a Duma, not simply to try and keep the liberals happy. He had now formed an alliance with Britain and France, and these two countries preferred Russia to have an elected parliament, just as they had. Therefore, a third Duma met. This time Stolypin changed the rules for voting, so that most peasants and industrial workers could not vote. This produced a Duma made up mainly of people who supported the tsar. As a result, it lasted for five years, from 1907 until 1912.

Source C Speech by the Octobrist leader Guchkov, in 1913

The attempt made by the Russian people to bring about a peaceful, painless transition from an old, condemned system to a new order has failed.

Source D A cartoon from a Russian magazine in 1906, showing a politician who represents the Duma, flanked by two representatives of the tsar.

Questions

1 Source **D** shows a Russian view of the Duma of 1906. Who does the man who is gagged and chained represent? Who do the other two men represent?

2 Why do you think that Guchkov (Source **C**) regarded the Dumas as a failure?

Agricultural reforms

Stolypin planned important changes in the countryside. Much of the violence of the 1905 Revolution had been carried out by peasants. To prevent another revolution in the future some of their demands would have to be met. However, Stolypin had another reason for introducing reforms. He wanted to turn Russia into a modern industrial country. For this to happen Russian agriculture would have to become more efficient, to produce the extra food which would be needed by the increasing numbers of industrial workers.

In November 1905, at the height of the Revolution, the tsar abolished redemption payments. This undoubtedly helped to reduce the anger of the peasants since many of them were no longer able to keep up their payments and so were afraid of losing their land.

In 1906 and 1907 Stolypin introduced measures which allowed peasants to leave the mir. The mir operated an open field system rather like England in the Middle Ages. Every village had a number of fields which were divided into long thin strips. Each family would have at least one strip in each field so that everyone got a share of the best and the worst land. However, this system was very inefficient.

- Time was wasted travelling between the strips;
- Everyone had to grow the same crop in each field;
- Strips were too small to encourage an ambitious peasant to buy machinery – most still used a wooden plough;
- Few animals were kept, so without manure to fertilise the land the mir used a rotation system – some of the fields were left fallow each year, and so produced no food at all.

Stolypin hoped that if peasants left the mir they would buy the strips around them and create efficient modern farms which would produce more food per hectare. Furthermore, these rich peasants or kulaks would want to spend their new wealth on consumer goods which would then stimulate Russian industrial production. Stolypin also believed that the kulaks would support the tsar, who had allowed them to become wealthy.

Source E The Mowers by Miasoyedov, painted in 1887. This picture shows Russian peasants working in the fields. Note the lack of any machinery.

Did Stolypin succeed?

Stolypin himself believed that it would take 20 years for these changes to work. However, he was assassinated in 1911 and later ministers were less committed to the new ideas than he had been. The outbreak of war in 1914 stopped them altogether.

Source F From a British school textbook, 1986

Millions of peasants bought their own land and set about creating new, efficient farms.

From Brooman *Russia in War and Revolution*, Longman 1986

Source G Russian agricultural statistics

Percentage of peasants who had left the mir by 1914	25%
Percentage of strip land which had been consolidated by 1916	10%

Source H Simplified plan of a typical Russian village in 1905

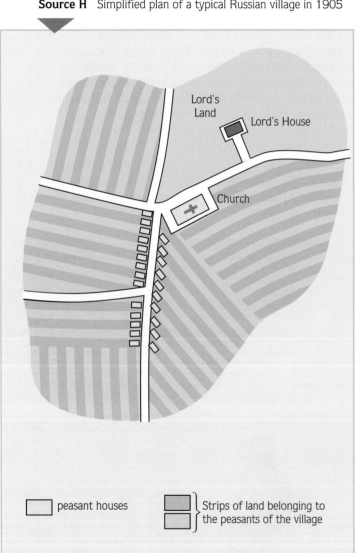

peasant houses

Strips of land belonging to the peasants of the village

Source I Simplified plan of a typical village in 1914

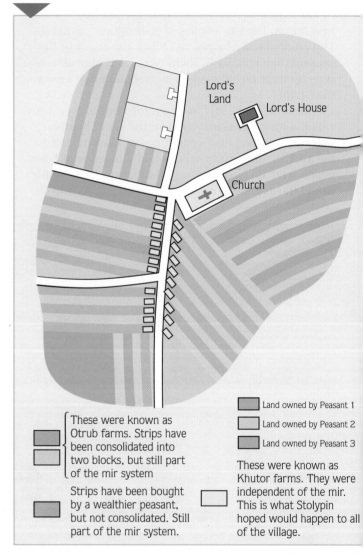

These were known as Otrub farms. Strips have been consolidated into two blocks, but still part of the mir system

Strips have been bought by a wealthier peasant, but not consolidated. Still part of the mir system.

Land owned by Peasant 1

Land owned by Peasant 2

Land owned by Peasant 3

These were known as Khutor farms. They were independent of the mir. This is what Stolypin hoped would happen to all of the village.

---

1 Why was open field farming inefficient?

2 Why did Stolypin want peasants to leave the mir?

3 Look at Sources **H** and **I** and the text.
   a) Do you think Stolypin would have been satisfied with peasant 1 and 2? Give your reasons.

b) Do you think Stolypin would have been satisfied with peasant 3? Give your reasons.

4 Do Sources **G** and **I** support the statement made in Source **F**?

Questions

Industry

Russia had made dramatic developments in modern industry in the late nineteenth century. However, there was a price to pay. Rapid industrialisation produced a middle class bourgeoisie who had no say in how the country was ruled and a proletariat who were forced to live and work in appalling conditions. The policy designed to make Russia successful also produced much of the discontent which led to the Revolution of 1905.

While the tsar and Stolypin hoped to buy the support of the bourgeoisie through the creation of the Duma, nothing was done to improve the conditions of industrial workers. When, in 1912, workers at the Lena gold-fields in Siberia went on strike for better wages and conditions, troops were sent in and 270 workers were killed and a further 250 injured.

Source J This textile mill on the River Volga shows that Russian industries used modern machinery.

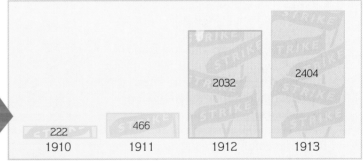

Source K
Bar chart of strikes in Russia 1910–13

222	466	2032	2404
1910	1911	1912	1913

Naval reform

Russia was a great power. Great powers were supposed to be able to defeat smaller powers. Yet this is what Russia had failed to do in the Japanese War of 1904 and 1905. Instead, they had been humiliated. For the navy it had been a total disaster. Of the three squadrons which made up the Russian navy, two had been completely destroyed and the other had mutinied. Weak leadership was blamed.

Far more power was therefore given to a single man, the naval minister, who worked closely with the Duma. Together they drew up a plan to build modern battleships which would have made Russia the third greatest naval power in the world by 1931. However, Russia lacked the money to do this more quickly, at a time that two other great powers – Britain and Germany – were engaged in a naval arms race which was producing huge battleships known as dreadnoughts.

Questions

1 Why should the Russian government have been worried by the figures in Source **K**?

2 What changes had taken place in Russia between 1905 and 1913? List the changes under four headings:
   a) Political changes
   b) Agricultural changes
   c) Industrial changes
   d) Military changes

3 What had not changed? Make a list using the same headings.

4 How successful had the Russian government been in dealing with the problems which faced it? Again use the same four headings that you used in Questions 2 and 3. In each case you will need to decide what the government was trying to achieve and whether it achieved that aim.

2 The end of the Old Order

The collapse of tsarist Russia

 Why did tsarism collapse in 1917?

The abdication of the tsar

Source A A message from Rodzianko, the leader of the Duma, to Tsar Nicholas, 27 February 1917

The transport system has broken down; the supply systems for food and fuel are completely disorganised. There is disorderly shooting in the streets; some of the troops are firing at each other.

Source B Nicholas' reaction to Rodzianko's message

The fat Rodzianko has sent me some nonsense. I shall not even bother to reply.

Despite the way in which he dismissed Rodzianko's message, just three days later Nicholas II abdicated as tsar. He handed over to his brother, Grand Duke Michael. Twenty-four hours later, Michael realised that Russia no longer wanted a tsar, and so he abdicated as well. After 304 years of ruling Russia, the Romanov family were giving up power. Just 12 years before, the tsar had survived the 1905 Revolution. Why did he fail to survive in 1917?

The First World War

On 1 August 1914, Russia went to war with Austria-Hungary and Germany. France and Great Britain joined on the Russian side. Just ten years after the disaster against Japan this was a great risk, but Russia was traditionally the defender of the Serbs. Austria-Hungary had declared war on Serbia and if Russia stood by and did nothing she would lose all influence in south-east Europe.

At first the war was very popular. It was assumed that the Russian 'steamroller' would crush the enemy. Russia's vast population meant that she could raise a much bigger army than anyone else. The reality turned out to be very different.

The Russian invasion of Germany was defeated and the Germans advanced into Russia. By the end of 1914 the Russians had lost over one million men either killed, wounded or captured. The retreat continued throughout 1915. Russia's huge army was ineffective. Although Russia began the war with 6 million troops, there were fewer than 5 million rifles. Many of the soldiers did not even have any boots. Perhaps most serious was the shortage of artillery shells, which meant that the Russians could not fire back when attacked.

Source C A group of people in Petrograd demonstrating in favour of the tsar and the war. The name of Petrograd had been adopted once the war began, because the name St. Petersburg sounded too German.

The Germans had forced us to retreat by artillery fire alone, using their enormous superiority in this field and their inexhaustible supplies of shells. As they were firing, our own batteries [artillery guns] had to remain silent even during serious clashes. As the enemy did not need to use its infantry [soldiers fighting on foot], they suffered hardly any casualties whilst our soldiers were dying by the thousand. Cases of desertion and of soldiers voluntarily giving themselves up to the enemy are becoming more frequent. It is difficult to expect selflessness and enthusiasm from men sent into battle without weapons and ordered to take rifles from their dead colleagues.

Source D Report by War Minister Polivanov, July 1915

Source E The circumstances leading to the outbreak of the First World War

Russia wanted to dominate the Balkans. Russia was also seen as the protector of the Slav peoples from Austro-Hungarian and Turkish aggression. Once Austro-Hungary was at war with Serbia, Russia had to attack Austro-Hungary. Russia was allied to France, and therefore any war with Russia would involve France as well.

The Austro-Hungarian Empire was made up of many different nationalities. Austria-Hungary wanted to keep Serbia weak to prevent the Serbs inside the Empire from wanting to join Serbia.

Germany was an ally of Austria-Hungary. Once Russia had declared war on Austria-Hungary, Germany was committed to war with Russia.

The Archduke Franz-Ferdinand of Austria was assassinated by a Serb when on a visit to Sarajevo. Austria-Hungary declared war on Serbia.

Ruled by Turkey, but made up of many nationalities. Attacked and largely captured by Serbia and Bulgaria in 1912.

GERMANY

RUSSIA

AUSTRIA-HUNGARY

ROMANIA

Sarajevo

BOSNIA

SERBIA

Black Sea

BULGARIA

MONTENEGRO

TURKEY IN EUROPE

TURKEY

GREECE

To make matters, worse the Russian army was led by officers who were chosen because they were nobles and not because they were good soldiers. Even the Germans were surprised by the numbers of Russians they were killing. The German commander General Hindenburg remarked 'In the great war book, the page on which the Russian losses were written has been torn out. No one knows the figures. All we know is that sometimes in our battles we had to remove the mounds of enemy corpses from in front of our trenches in order to get a clear field of fire against fresh attacking waves of Russians.'

In 1905 the troops who returned from the war with Japan had remained loyal to the tsar and put down the revolt. After the horrors they were suffering in this war some people felt that they would not do so again.

Source F
Wounded Russian soldiers, 1916

Questions

1 What is meant by the term 'Russian steamroller'?

2 Look at Source **D**. Why did the Russian steamroller not work in the First World War?

The effects of the war

Social and economic effects

Source G   Numbers of Russian railway engines in working order

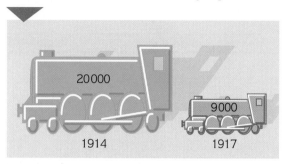

Source H   The population of Moscow, 1914–17

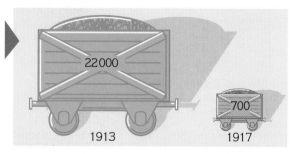

Source I   Wagons of grain reaching Moscow, 1913–17

While the war went badly for the Russians on the battlefields, there were important effects on the rest of Russia. During the war, over 15 million young men were called up for the armed forces. This meant that there were not enough peasants to grow the food for both the army and the workers in the towns. However, the situation was more complicated than this. As the Russian army retreated, it abandoned huge areas of territory to the advancing Germans. The people who lived in these areas fled to the Russian cities. So there were more hungry mouths to feed. Yet Source **I** shows there was less and less food to feed them.

Food could only reach the cities by rail, but the railways were being used to move military equipment for the army. Therefore food rotted in railway sidings while people starved in the cities. The situation became even worse in 1916. Factories only produced materials for the war, and so there was nothing for peasants to buy with the money they earned from selling their crops. Therefore, more and more peasants only grew enough for themselves to eat. There was no point in producing a surplus to sell.

Between 1914 and 1917 inflation in Russia rose by almost 400 per cent. The workers found that their wages did not keep pace and so they could afford very little of the food which was available. The result was unrest in the cities as hundreds of thousands of workers went on strike.

Political effects

In August 1915 the tsar took personal command of the army and went to live at the army headquarters. This was a serious mistake. Every failure of the army would now be blamed on the tsar. The government was left in the hands of the tsarina, and she was influenced by the unpopular Rasputin (see the biography box). She was also a German, and this led many people to believe that Russia was now in the hands of the enemy.

The tsar made the situation worse by refusing the help of elected bodies, such as the Union of Zemstva and the Union of Town Councils. Together they formed ZEMGOR, which carried out excellent work helping casualties from the war, in complete contrast to the government's own efforts. Yet when they offered to help in other areas, such as ensuring the army was well supplied, Nicholas turned them down. In the same way, although he called a Duma in 1915, he refused their offer to provide him with a new government of elected politicians, to replace his own incompetent cabinet. The majority of the Duma formed the 'Progressive Bloc'. At first they just wanted to try to convince the tsar to adopt their policies and replace his cabinet. The tsar would not listen to them. The only way to change the government was to change the tsar, which is how the tsar found himself in a railway carriage at Pskov, signing the decree of abdication.

The February Revolution in Petrograd

The events of the February Revolution actually lasted from 18 February 1917 to 3 March. Yet it was hardly a planned revolution. Tsarism simply collapsed. There was no one willing to save it.

The Russian Calendar

Under the tsars, Russia used the Julian calendar. This was 13 days behind the Gregorian calendar, which is used in the West. On 14 February 1918 Lenin announced that Russia was to adopt the Gregorian calendar, which meant that 1 February became 14 February. This means that the February Revolution can also be called the March Revolution!

Rasputin

Rasputin was a monk and the son of a Siberian peasant. His real name was Grigory Yefimovich, but he gained the nickname of Rasputin, meaning 'immoral'.

The tsarina believed that Rasputin was a miracle worker since he seemed to be able to cure her son's haemophilia. However, Rasputin also lived up to his nickname, taking part in orgies and reportedly sleeping with many of the leading women of the court.

The situation became critical after August 1915, once

▶ Rasputin surrounded by admirers

the tsar had taken control of the army. The tsarina was left in charge of the government and totally under the influence of Rasputin. Men were given posts in government not because they were good at their job but simply because they knew how to please Rasputin.

Finally, in December 1916, a group of nobles killed Rasputin. They believed that they were saving Russia, but Rasputin's death changed little. He was a symptom, not a cause of the problem.

Source J From *The History of the Russian Revolution*, by Trotsky, Chairman of the Petrograd soviet

One half of the industrial workers of Petrograd are on strike on 24 February. The workers come to the factories in the morning; instead of going to work they hold meetings; then begin processions towards the centre. The slogan 'Bread' is drowned out by louder slogans: 'Down with autocracy!' 'Down with the war!'.

Around the barracks and lines of soldiers stood groups of working men and women exchanging friendly words with the army men.

Source L From the diary of Louis de Robien, a French diplomat and eyewitness

Serious mutiny has broken out among the troops and all the men we saw belong to regiments sent to restore order, who, after firing a few shots, joined the mutineers.

Source M Soldiers on the streets after the tsar's abdication in February 1917

Source K By Dmitri Shakhovskoi, a 14 year-old eyewitness

Terrible things are happening in Petrograd. Gunfire never ceases in our part of the city. The officers cannot go into the streets, because the crowd disarms them, molests them and even kills them.

Questions

1 Look at Source **H**. Why did the population of Moscow increase during the war?

2 Look at Sources **G** and **I** and the text. How far does Source **G** explain the lack of food shown by Source **I**? What other reasons can you find?

3 **a)** Look at Sources **G**, **H** and **I**. What reasons do they suggest for the fall of the tsar?
b) Look at Sources **J**, **K** and **L**. What other reasons do they suggest for the fall of the tsar?
c) Write the answers to **a)** and **b)** on a grid like the one below and then tick whether you feel these reasons are social, political or military.

Reason	Social	Political	Military

4 What do you think the phrase 'He was a symptom, not a cause of the problem' means when used about Rasputin?

5 **a)** Use the grid from Question 3. Turn back to pages 14–17 and write in the causes of the 1905 Revolution.
b) Which reasons for the fall of the tsar in 1917 are not on your grid as reasons for the 1905 revolution?
c) Why do you think the revolution of 1905 failed, but the revolution of February 1917 succeeded? Use your grid to help you.

The story of the Provisional Government

Anti-war demonstration in Petrograd

May
Guchkov, the Minister of War, and Milyukov, the Foreign Minister, were forced to resign from the Provisional Government because they wanted to fight the war to the end, not just until the Germans had been driven from Russian soil.

June
A new Russian offensive is launched against the Germans in an attempt to drive them out of Russia. It is a disaster, with 60 000 Russian troops killed.

July
The failure of the offensive produced the 'July Days'. The Bolsheviks lead demonstrations demanding the overthrow of the Provisional Government. Troops loyal to the government put down the protest. Trotsky was arrested and Lenin fled to Finland. Kerensky became the new prime minister. Kerensky called the Bolsheviks 'German traitors'.

July Days

April
Lenin arrived at Finland Railway Station in Petrograd after being transported to Russia by the Germans. He ordered all Bolsheviks to oppose the Provisional Government. In the months that followed his ideas were summed up in the slogans 'Peace, Bread and Land' and 'All Power to the Soviets'.

Lenin addressing crowds of supporters at Finland station

The **Provisional Government** which took over from the tsar were members of the Duma's 'Progressive Bloc' (see page 24). As their name suggested, they were a temporary government until elections were held to form a parliament which draw up a new system of laws for Russia. Some of the first actions of the Provisional Government were very popular:
* Political prisoners were freed.
* An eight-hour day was introduced for industrial workers.
* The tsar's secret police was abolished.

The first prime minister was Prince Lvov, but in July 1917 Alexander Kerensky took over. He was a Social Revolutionary (see page 10) and a member of the Petrograd soviet and was extremely popular with the workers and soldiers.

1 War
The Provisional Government decided to carry on fighting the First World War. Russia was bankrupt, and only by continuing to fight the war would the Western Allies pump more money into Russia. Another Russian attack in June 1917 was defeated and 60 000 more Russian troops were killed. The Provisional Government was caught in a terrible crisis. They felt they could only last as long as they continued to fight the war, yet the war was making them very unpopular.

March
* Provisional Government and Petrograd soviet established in the Tauride Palace.
* Soviet issues Order No. 1.

All soldiers and sailors were ordered to set up committees to take control of all weapons and equipment. It was obeyed throughout the army and meant that the soviet, and not the Provisional Government, controlled the Russian armed forces.

August

The new commander of the army, General Kornilov, attempted to take power by capturing Petrograd. Kerensky allowed the Bolshevik leaders to return to Petrograd to successfully organise resistance and defeat Kornilov. The Bolsheviks were now heroes and not traitors.

Kornilov

September

The Bolsheviks became the largest group in the Petrograd soviet. Trotsky was elected leader of the Petrograd soviet.

October

Lenin returned to Petrograd. The Petrograd soviet created the Military Revolutionary Committee with Trotsky as its head. In theory it was set up to defend the soviet, but in reality it allowed Trotsky to control the troops in Petrograd and plan a Bolshevik take-over of power in the name of the Petrograd soviet.

Trotsky

25–27 October

The Bolsheviks seize power in Petrograd.

2 Land

The peasants expected the Provisional Government to give them land that had previously belonged to the Church and the nobles. Since most of the supporters of the Provisional Government were members of the landowning class, they could not agree to this. In many parts of Russia the peasants took the law into their own hands and seized the land of local landlords for themselves. Many soldiers deserted from the army to return home so that they would not miss out on their share of the land. The violence in the countryside delayed the harvesting and this increased the food shortages.

3 Dual authority

The unelected Provisional Government met in the Tauride Palace in Petrograd. In the same building was the Petrograd Soviet of Workers and Soldiers Deputies. As its name suggests, this council had been elected by the workers and soldiers of the Petrograd area.

At first, the Provisional Government and the Petrograd soviet worked closely together, but gradually they grew further apart. In particular, the soviet increasingly came under the influence of the Bolsheviks, who were opposed to the war. This was not just because more Bolsheviks were elected to the soviet, but also because fewer members of the other parties chose to attend its endless meetings.

The storming of the Winter Palace

Questions

1 Why was the Provisional Government unwilling to end the war?

2 Why was Order No. 1 such a serious blow for the Provisional Government?

3 What evidence could the prime minister, Kerensky, use to back up his accusation that the Bolsheviks were 'German traitors'?

The fall of the Provisional Government

▶ **Why was the Provisional Government in power for such a short time?**

The importance of Lenin

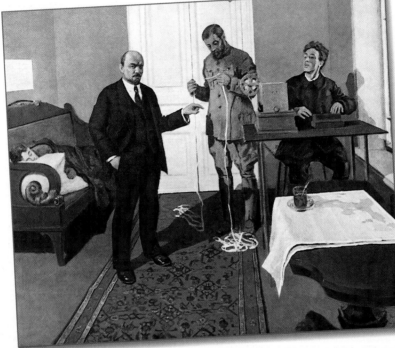

Lenin arrived in Petrograd on 3 April 1917, having secretly crossed Europe in a train provided by the Germans. One German official compared Lenin to a deadly virus which would infect Russia and lead to German victory in the war.

'The vanguard of the proletariat'

Until Lenin returned, the Bolsheviks had been working with other revolutionary groups to support the Provisional Government. They believed that the February Revolution was a bourgeois revolution, as predicted by Marx (see page 12). They thought it would not be possible for a proletarian revolution to happen until this stage was complete. Lenin disagreed, and eventually managed to convince the other leading Bolsheviks. He declared that the February Revolution was not a revolution at all. Power was still in the hands of the same class – the landlords.

With the slogan 'All power to the soviets' Lenin showed that he did not want a parliamentary government. He knew that the Bolsheviks did not have enough support to be influential in such a system. Instead, he wanted the Bolsheviks to gain control of the soviets, so that they could perform their role as 'the vanguard of the proletariat' (see page 11).

The support of the peasants

Lenin had been opposed to the war from the very beginning. He described the bayonet as a weapon with a worker at both ends. His slogan 'Peace, Bread and Land' expressed the desires of ordinary people. They wanted more food and an end to the killing of their friends and relatives. However, the presence of the word 'land' in this slogan shows another way in which Lenin was important. He could adapt his ideas to changing circumstances.

Before April 1917, the Bolsheviks had disregarded the peasants. Trotsky has described the peasants as 'the pack animals of history'. Now that he was back in Russia, Lenin could see that the peasants were playing a leading role in the revolution, seizing land from the landowners. Therefore, Lenin simply stole the land policy of the Social Revolutionaries (see page 10) and promised that all land would be divided among the peasants. This meant that at least the peasants would not oppose the Bolsheviks when they took power.

It was Lenin who provided the Bolsheviks' popular policies and the determination to take power. Without Lenin, the Bolsheviks would have supported parliamentary elections and would not have planned a revolution for many years.

Source B By Guchkov, the Minister of War, March 1917

The Provisional Government has no real force at its disposal, and its orders are carried out only to the extent that is permitted by the Soviet of Workers and Soldiers' Deputies which has in its hands the most important elements of real power – the army, the railways, the post and telegraphs.

Source C Petrograd Soviet Order No. 1

The orders of the military commission of the state Duma [Provisional Government] are to be obeyed only in such instances when they do not contradict the orders of the soviet.

Source D Daily bread rations for Russian workers in 1917

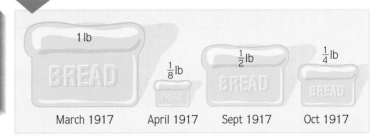

1 lb — March 1917
$\frac{1}{8}$ lb — April 1917
$\frac{1}{2}$ lb — Sept 1917
$\frac{1}{4}$ lb — Oct 1917

Source E An extract from an article in the Russian newspaper 'The Citizen Soldier', 1917

'To the end!' shout the agents of the allied governments while touring the battlefields strewn with the bodies of the workers. Can the soldiers in the trenches cry 'War to the end!'? No. He says something else.
Until the end of the war we'll be without food.
Until the end of the war Russia won't be free.

Source F The flight of Kerensky, painted in 1936–8

Questions

1 Why do you think that Guchkov (Source **B**) felt that it was so important that the Petrograd soviet controlled 'the army, the railways, the post and telegraph'?

2 Does Source **C** support what Guchkov is saying in Source **B**? Explain your answer.

3 How does Source **E** help to explain why Guchkov and Milyukov resigned in May 1917?

4 Sources **A** and **F** were both painted by Bolshevik supporters in the late 1930s. What impressions are they trying to give of Lenin and Kerensky?

5 Sources **A** and **F** were both painted almost 20 years after the events which they show. Does this mean they are of no use to the historian? Explain why you agree or disagree.

6 How does Source **D** help to explain why the war led to the fall of the Provisional Government?

7 Why was it important to Lenin that the Bolsheviks did not support the Provisional Government?

8 **a)** Make a list of all the causes you can think of which led to the fall of the Provisional Government.
b) Choose the **three** you consider to be the most important and explain why.
c) Draw up a table with two columns. Head the first column 'Weaknesses of the Provisional Government' and the second 'Strengths of the Bolsheviks'. Place as many causes from **a)** as you can into one or other of these columns. (Not all of your causes will be relevant.)

9 Was the fall of the Provisional Government due to its own weaknesses or to the strengths of the Bolsheviks? Use the table from Question 8 to help you.

The October Revolution

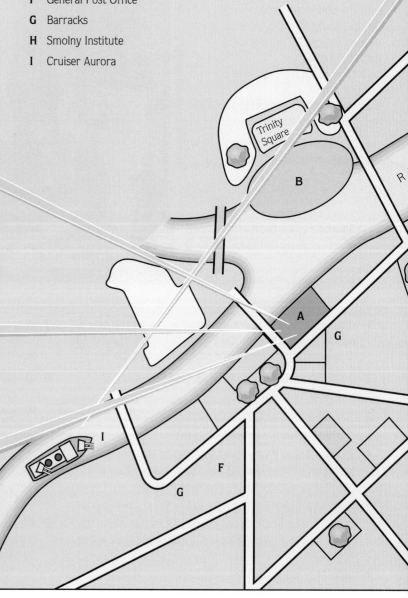

7

Night of 24–25 October
Bolsheviks launch the revolution, seizing bridges and the Post Office.

5

The Winter Palace, Provisional Government Headquarters
Night of 23–24 October
Kerensky sends troops to close down two Bolshevik newspapers, 'Pravda' and 'Izvesta', However, Kerensky's troops are beaten off by troops sent by the MRC.

9

The Winter Palace
About 11a.m.
Kerensky leaves the Winter Palace to try and contact troops loyal to the Provisional Government and bring them into Petrograd to help defeat the Bolsheviks.

10

About 11.30p.m.
The 'Aurora' fires on the Winter Palace and the Bolshevik attack begins. The palace is only defended by cadets and a women's unit. At 1.30 a.m. the Provisional Government are captured. Only six people died in the attack.

A   The Winter Palace
B   Peter and Paul Fortress
C   Finland Station
D   Nicholas Station
E   Tauride Palace
F   General Post Office
G   Barracks
H   Smolny Institute
I   Cruiser Aurora

6

24 October
Ships supporting the Bolsheviks led by the cruiser 'Aurora', arrive from Kronstadt Naval Base and train their guns on the city.

4

Peter and Paul Fortress
Garrison agree to support the Bolsheviks and give them weapons. On 23 October Trotsky reports that 15 of the 18 armed units in the capital support a seizure of power by the Bolsheviks.

2

On 7 October Lenin returns to Petrograd. On 10 October, in a secret meeting, he manages to convince a majority of the Bolshevik leadership to support an armed seizure of power.

1

Smolny Institute, Headquarters of Petrograd soviet
September
Bolsheviks become majority party in Petrograd soviet. Trotsky is elected Chairman of the soviet.

3

Smolny Institute
The Petrograd soviet creates a Military Revolutionary Committee (MRC), under the control of Trotsky. This means that Trotsky can now organise a Bolshevik revolution under the legal authority of the Petrograd soviet.

8

Smolny Institute
10 a.m.
Lenin issues a statement which is plastered on walls all over Petrograd– 'The Provisional Government is no more and power has passed to the soviets'.

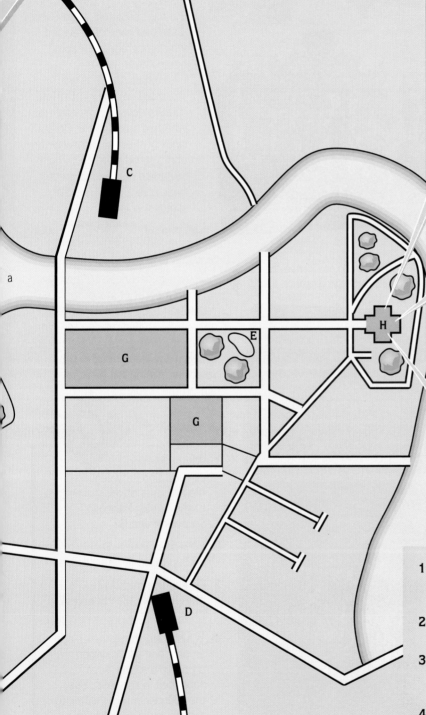

Questions

1 Using all 10 boxes, briefly list the events of the October Revolution in the correct chronological order.

2 Why do you think so few troops were willing to defend the Provisional Government?

3 Why did Lenin announce that the Provisional Government had been defeated before it was actually true?

4 Why did the Bolsheviks claim to be carrying out the revolution on behalf of the Petrograd soviet?

Eisenstein's film **October** as an historical source

Source A A still from the film *October*, showing the storming of the Winter Palace. This film was made in 1927.

Lenin regarded films as the most important art form. In a nation with so many people who could not read, the cinema offered a tremendous opportunity to spread Bolshevik ideas. In October 1917 there were already 1000 cinemas in Russia and the Bolsheviks added to these with 'agit-trains', which toured the country showing propaganda films in areas without cinemas. The famous Bolshevik film director was Sergei Eisenstein. His most famous films were *Potemkin*, about the naval mutiny in the 1905 Revolution, and *October*, about the October Revolution.

Source B An eyewitness account of the storming of the Winter Palace by an American, John Reed

It was absolutely dark. Over the barricade of firewood we clambered, and leaping down inside gave a triumphant shout as we stumbled on a heap of rifles thrown down by the soldiers who had stood there. On both sides of the main gateway the doors stood wide open, light streamed out, and from the huge palace came not the slightest sound.

Source C A painting of the storming of the Winter Palace. This picture was produced in the 1920s in the socialist realist style (see page 52).

Source D From *Timewatch*, a BBC television programme, 1987

Cameras at that time couldn't shoot in darkness, so there are no contemporary films of the revolution. Eisenstein used live ammunition when making the film *October*. More people were injured and more damage done to the palace in making the film than during the revolution itself.

Questions

1 What differences can you find between the accounts of the storming of the Winter Palace in Sources **A** and **B**?

2 How does Source **D** help to explain these differences?

3 Do you believe Source **C** is more reliable than Source **A**? Give reasons.

4 'A historian should never rely on only one source when trying to discover what happened in the past'. Use the sources in this chapter to explain why you agree or disagree with this statement.

The creation of the first communist state

Holding on to power

 How did the Bolsheviks manage to establish control of the Russian Empire?

The Bolsheviks in power

The Bolsheviks had won. Yet in many ways their problems had only just begun. Russia needed strong government. Lenin himself took command and formed SOVNARCOM – the Council of Peoples Commissars. This small group of leading Bolsheviks now ran the country.

Opposition to the Bolsheviks was made as difficult as opposition to the Tsar had been in the past. All non-Bolshevik newspapers were banned and in December 1917 a secret police force, the Cheka, was set up. The purpose of the Cheka was to stop anyone overthrowing the Bolsheviks. Its leader, Felix Dzerzhinsky, proclaimed 'We stand for organised terror'. It is estimated that the Cheka killed more than 250 000 people between 1917 and 1924.

The Bolsheviks were faced with a series of problems which had to be solved if they were to remain in power – land ownership, the Constituent Assembly and how to end the war.

Land

According to Marx, no one would own property in a communist society. Everything would be shared. Yet since the February Revolution the peasants had been taking land for themselves. The Bolsheviks could not reverse what had happened. If they tried, the peasants would probably revolt.

Therefore, one of the first laws issued by the new government was the Decree on Land:

> 'Private ownership of land shall be abolished for ever. All land shall be confiscated without compensation and become the property of the whole people and pass into the use of those who cultivate it.'

This appears to follow the Marxist line, but in reality allowed the peasants to keep the land which they'd taken from the landlords. This is a further example of the realism that made Lenin such an effective leader. He had a very clear idea of what was possible and what was not. Lenin took decisions based on their likely consequences, rather than blindly following what Marx had said.

The Constituent Assembly

There was also the problem of the Constituent Assembly. Before the Revolution in October, all political parties, including the Bolsheviks, had been calling for this to meet. The Provisional Government had finally

Source A The Constituent Assembly

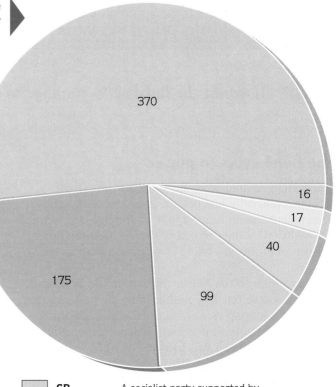

set the election date for November. The Assembly's job would be to draw up a new constitution – a new set of rules by which Russia would be governed.

However, now that he had seized power, Lenin did not want an assembly to decide how Russia was to be ruled. He would do that. The Constituent Assembly finally met on 5 January (Old Calendar) 1918. Yet after just one day Lenin ordered Bolshevik troops to stop people from entering the Tauride Palace, where the Assembly met. At the same time, two Kadet leaders were murdered in a hospital by bands of sailors. Chernov, the leader of the Social Revolutionaries, organised a peaceful protest, but this was easily ended by armed Bolsheviks.

If the supporters of the Constituent Assembly were to get their way, they would have to use force. Many joined the 'White' forces which sought to overthrow the Bolsheviks in the civil war (see page 37).

SR	A socialist party supported by the peasants
Bolsheviks	The only Socialist Party to oppose the war
National	Made up of various national minority groups
Left SR	Socialist Party who split from the SRs to support the Bolsheviks
Kadets	Wanted liberal parliamentary democracy, not socialism
Mensheviks	Socialist Party who split from the Bolsheviks

Figures show number of seats won in Assembly

Source C By C. Lindhagen, a Swedish eyewitness in the Tauride Palace

In one of the corridors leading from the hall, a group of armed soldiers could be glimpsed. I was informed that several of the deputies as well as the commissars were armed. I asked one commissar at random whether this was true. 'Of course,' he replied, and showed me the butt of a revolver in his trouser pocket. A second person told me that for the sake of fairness supporters of all parties had been allowed into the public galleries. I realised that it was possible that a bomb might be thrown from the public gallery.

Source D By Chernov, the Social Revolutionary leader

When we entered the Tauride Palace, where the assembly met on January 18 1918, we found that the corridors were full of armed guards. Every sentence of my speech was met with outcries, some spiteful, often supported by the brandishing of guns. Lenin demonstrated his contempt for the Assembly by lounging in his chair and giving the impression of a man who was bored to death.

Question

1 Look at Source **B**.
   a) Which party won the most seats in the new Constituent Assembly?
   b) Why do you think they did so well?
   c) Does any one party hold more seats than all of the other parties put together?
   d) How many seats are held by socialist parties?
   e) What sort of government do you think that the Constituent Assembly would have demanded?
   f) Why would Lenin have been opposed to this?

2 Does Source **A** or Source **D** give you a fuller picture of the events of 5 January? Why do you think this is?

3 Does Source **C** give you any information not in Source **D**?

4 Do you feel that Source **C** or Source **D** is the more reliable? Give your reasons.

The end of the war

Perhaps the most serious problem the Bolsheviks had to deal with was how to get out of the First World War. From the moment that war had broken out, Lenin had opposed it on the grounds that the working people of the world should not be fighting and killing one another. He felt that the war was started by the wealthy bourgeoisie who simply wanted to conquer land to make themselves richer.

Now he was in power, Lenin realised that the war must be ended if the Bolsheviks were to hold on to power. The strains of the war had destroyed both the tsarist regime and the Provisional Government, but Lenin was determined that it would not do the same to the Bolsheviks.

Source F The heaped up bodies of Russian soldiers in 1918

The Bolsheviks met the Germans at Brest-Litovsk, a town just behind the German front line. Lenin was willing to give the Germans almost as much land as they wanted in order to buy peace as quickly as possible. This was an incredibly difficult decision for Lenin to make. He had already been accused of being a German spy when he accepted German help to get to Petrograd in April 1917. Now he risked being called a traitor once more for handing over Russian territory to the Germans.

Trotsky wanted to delay the peace negotiations because he believed the example of the Russian revolution would inspire the workers of Germany to overthrow their government. However, the German commanders became frustrated with Trotsky's

Source E The Treaty of Brest-Litovsk

0   km   500

N

Baltic Sea
GERMANY
ESTONIA
LATVIA
LITHUANIA
● Petrograd
Moscow ●
BYELO-RUSSIA
UKRAINE
AUSTRIA-HUNGARY
Black Sea
GEORGIA
T U R K E Y

Russia lost:

26% of her population

27% of her arable land

26% of her railway mileage

74% of her iron ore and coal

- - - - Russia's frontier after the Treaty of Brest-Litovsk

—— Russia's 1914 frontier

Territory lost at Brest-Litovsk which the Russians did not regain in the Civil War.

Territory lost at Brest-Litovsk which the Russians did regain in the Civil War.

Enemies of Russia in the First World War

delaying tactics, and so they attacked the Russian army again. Lenin realised that the Russian army was too weak to defeat the Germans, so there was nothing to lose by giving them everything they wanted. If the Germans won the war they would take this land anyway. On the other hand, if the Germans eventually lost the war to Britain, the Russians would be able to regain all the land they had given away. Most Russians, even some Bolsheviks, were horrified by the amount of land which Lenin and Trotsky gave away in March 1918 at Brest-Litovsk (see Source **E**). Russia also had to pay Germany 3 billion roubles as compensation. Yet Lenin's gamble seemed to pay off. Eight months later, Germany was defeated by Britain and America. German troops then withdrew from the occupied areas of the Russian Empire.

Source G Decree on Peace, issued by the Bolshevik Government in November 1918

The workers' and peasants' government proposes to all the warring peoples and their governments that they immediately enter into talks for a just peace. This sort of peace would be an immediate peace without seizure of foreign territory and without financial penalties.

It will be a good thing if the German proletariat revolt. But can you predict that the German revolution will break out on a specific day ? If the revolution breaks out, everything is saved. But if it does not, what then?

Our impulse is to refuse to sign this robber peace. Russia can offer no resistance because she is materially exhausted by three years of war. It is true that there may still be people who are willing to fight and die for a great cause. Wars are won today, not by enthusiasm alone, but by technical skill, railways and abundant supplies. Russia must sign the peace to obtain breathing space to recuperate for the struggle.

Source J Russian soldier threatening two deserters

Comintern

Holding on to power in Russia was only the first stage in the process. Lenin believed that capitalism was ready to be overthrown by socialism in every country, not only in Russia. Therefore, in March 1919 he established Comintern or the Third International.

Comintern's purpose was to organise Socialist revolutions across Europe. As its name suggests, this was not a new idea. Socialists had long been trying to work together to organise a future international revolution. The Second International had collapsed with the outbreak of the First World War as many socialists, unlike Lenin, had supported their own countries in the fighting. The very existence of Comintern made sure that western countries such as Britain and America would want the Bolsheviks to lose power in Russia, since the Bolsheviks were trying to encourage the workers in these countries to overthrow their own governments.

Source K Russian poster promoting Comintern

Questions

1 Were Bolshevik hopes for the 'just peace' in Source **G** realised in the Treaty of Brest-Litovsk?

2 What problems faced by the Bolsheviks are shown by Sources **F** and **J**?

3 In what ways does Source **E** support the view that Lenin's gamble at Brest-Litovsk was successful?

4 Many of the leading Bolsheviks opposed the signing of the Treaty of Brest-Litovsk. Look at Source **H**. What argument must they have been using?

5 Do you think that signing the Treaty of Brest-Litovsk was a success for the Russians?

The civil war

▶ **Why was there a civil war?**
Why did the Bolsheviks win?

Reds and Whites

It was hardly surprising that a civil war broke out in Russia after the Bolsheviks, or REDS, seized power. Many people did not want to see the Bolsheviks stay in power. Those who opposed the Bolsheviks were known as the WHITES, although they were never a united group, and they had little in common except a hatred of the Bolsheviks.

Parties such as the Social Revolutionaries and the Kadets wanted the Constituent Assembly back to decide the future of Russia. Other people wanted the tsar to rule again. Landowners were angry because peasants were allowed to keep the land they had taken.

Foreign countries such as Britain, America and France knew that if Russia withdrew from the war then the full might of the German army would be turned onto their armies on the Western Front. Therefore these countries sent troops to Russia as well as giving huge quantities of arms, including tanks and aircraft, to the White armies. This was because the Whites promised to continue to fight the Germans once they were in power. These Whites united behind former generals of the tsar such as Denikin, Kolchak, Wrangel and Yudenich.

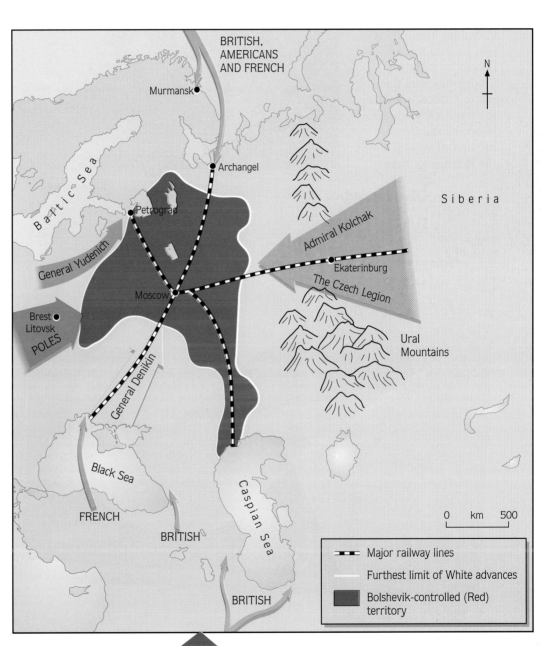

Source A A map of the civil war

The Czech Legion

The presence of the Czech Legion in Russia added to the confusion. Many of the Czech Legion had fought for the Russians in the First World War in the hope that a new state of Czechoslovakia would be created if Germany and Austria were defeated. Some were prisoners of war captured in the fighting.

After the Treaty of Brest-Litovsk, the Bolsheviks promised to send the Czechs to France to continue fighting the Germans. The only way was to send the 50 000 Czechs by train to Vladivostok and then by sea to France, a journey of considerable length. However, the Czechs became suspicious that the Bolsheviks were going to hand them over to the Germans, especially after Trotsky ordered that all Czechs who refused to give up their weapons would be shot. The Czech Legion then seized control of the Trans-Siberian Railway and began to head back towards Moscow intent on defeating the Reds. During 1918 they were probably the most effective White army, and they succeeded in driving the Red Army out of Siberia.

Source B A Bolshevik poster of 1919. Former generals of the tsar – Denikin, Kolchak and Yudenich – are shown on the ground and already defeated. Another White general, Wrangel, is pulling a cart containing the bourgeoisie, a landowner and the tsar.

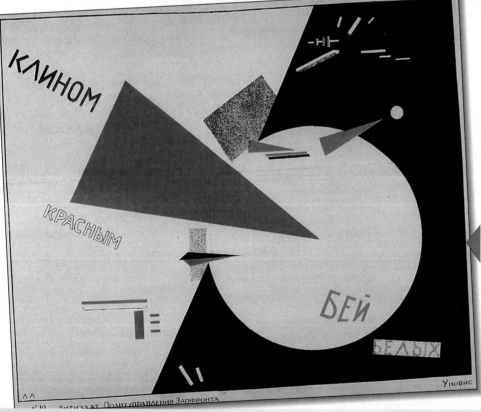

Source C A Bolshevik poster of 1920 – Defeat the Whites with the Red Wedge

Questions

1 The tsars had spent only 4 per cent of the country's budget on education. Does this help explain why the Bolsheviks used posters to put their message across?

2 Sources **B** and **C** were both published by the Bolsheviks during the civil war.
   a) Which of these sources do you think is most useful to historians who are:

   • studying the attitude of the Bolsheviks to their enemies?
   • studying the types of propaganda used by the Bolsheviks?

   b) What makes a source useful to the historian? Use Sources **B** and **C** to back up your answer.

Why were the Reds able to win the civil war?

During 1918 the Red Army was on the retreat and the Bolsheviks were threatened on all sides, as Source **A** shows. Yet, despite being greatly outnumbered both in men and equipment, by 1921 the Red Army had defeated the White armies. Why was this?

● The Whites were not organised into a single army, but operated as a number of independent forces. Therefore, although in Source **A** the Reds appear to be surrounded and fighting on six fronts at once, this was not really the case. In fact the Whites attacked separately, so the Red Army was able to deal with them one at a time.

● The Reds had a geographical advantage. They controlled the central area of Russia, where there were good railways. This meant the Reds could move troops quickly and keep in close touch with their armies. By contrast the Whites were scattered over a huge area and found it very difficult to keep in contact.

● The Reds made sure that all possible resources were diverted to the army, even if this led to suffering among the peasants and factory workers. This was known as War Communism (see page 44).

Source D Denikin, Kolchak and Yudenich on leads controlled by Britain, France and America

The new Red Army

Trotsky became Commissar for War and reorganised the Red Army. He took a number of decisions which were very unpopular with many Bolsheviks, but which turned the Red Army into an effective fighting force. The old Russian army had almost collapsed with the introduction of the Petrograd Soviet's Order No. 1.

There was little discipline, as the men elected their own officers and capital punishment was banned. Trotsky restored capital punishment and employed many of the best officers from the tsar's army. To ensure they remained loyal to the Bolsheviks members of their family were often taken hostage. Each officer was accompanied by a loyal Bolshevik party member, known as a 'politruk'. No officer could issue an order unless it was also signed by a 'politruk'.

Trotsky also promoted talented soldiers who had never been made officers in the noblity-dominated tsarist army. These men, such as Tuchachevsky and Zhukov, became the Red Army's best generals. Conscription was introduced to enlarge the Red Army to five million.

Trotsky constantly visited the front line troops, raising morale with his speeches which told the troops exactly what they were fighting for. In contrast, morale among White forces was much lower, and they suffered from large numbers of men deserting in many battles.

Questions

1 a) Make a list of the differences between the way the Red Army and the old tsarist army were organised.
   b) Make a list of those things which were the same.

2 The Bolsheviks had promised to give power to the people and to destroy the power of the rich.
   a) Do you think that all Bolshevik supporters would have agreed with the changes that Trotsky made to the Red Army?
   b) Which changes would they have liked and which would they not have liked? Give your reasons.

3 Source **B** shows a landowner on the cart. Do you think that the peasants would support the Reds or the Whites? Give your reasons.

4 Here are five reasons for the Red victory in the civil war:
   · *Trotsky's reorganisation of the Red Army* · *White disunity* · *Geography* · *Patriotism* · *Peasant support*
   a) Comment briefly on the importance of each factor.
   b) Explain which you think is the most important reason for the Bolshevik victory.

Source E Trotsky on his special train which he used to tour the battlefields to encourage the troops

39

What happened to the tsar and his family?

Source A The British and Russian royal families at Cowes on the Isle of Wight, 1909

After his abdication in February 1917, the tsar and his family were allowed to live in the royal palace at Tsarskoye Selo. This was close to Petrograd and the Provisional Government became afraid that the family were so unpopular that they might be attacked by the local people. Therefore, they were moved to Tobolsk in Siberia. Then, in April 1918, as the White armies gained control of Siberia, the Bolshevik government moved them to Ekaterinburg in the Ural Mountains. After this, they just seemed to disappear. What did happen to the tsar and his family? It is your task to look at the evidence presented here, and decide what you think really happened. Source **C** gives the standard textbook account and Source **D** shows a contemporary picture of what is thought to have happened.

Source B Tsar Nicholas and his family under arrest at Tobolsk

Source C By J.N. Westwood, in a British textbook published in 1973

In the summer of 1918 the civil war was not going well and it seemed that the White forces would soon capture Ekaterinburg. Although there was time to remove the royal family it would appear that the decision was taken to kill them. The eleven victims at Ekaterinburg were the tsar and his family, together with their four servants. The official announcement of the execution of Nicholas declared that the empress and the children had been 'sent to a safe place'. This deception was because the government believed that it was on the brink of war with Germany; to announce the execution of the empress (a German princess) would only have increased the danger. The bodies were taken to a deserted mine shaft, chopped up, burned, and the remains strewn in marshland.

Source D The execution of the tsar. A painting by Sarmet, a White supporter.

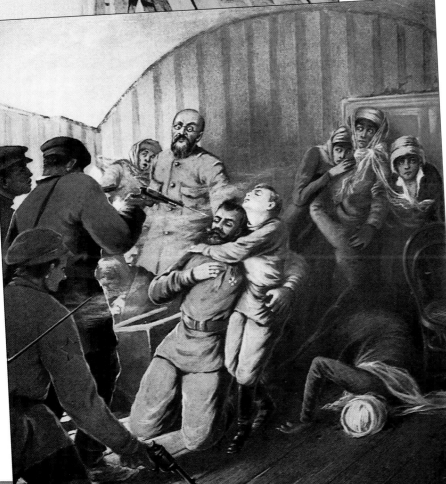

How do we know that the account in Source **C** is true? There were no bodies to prove that the family were dead. Source **C** is relying on an investigation carried out by the Whites after they captured Ekaterinburg. However, the investigator, Sokolov, did not arrive in the town until February 1919, many months after the royal family had disappeared. Sokolov based his conclusions on two pieces of evidence:

1 The account of Pavel Medvedev (Source **E**), a Bolshevik who had been guarding the family;
2 The bullet-ridden room in which the murders were supposedly carried out (Source **H**).

Source E By Pavel Medvedev, a Bolshevik who gave himself up to the White forces in February 1919

When I entered the room all the prisoners were lying on the ground, in various positions, in the midst of enormous pools of blood. All were dead apart from Alexei, who was still moaning. Before my eyes Yurovsky (the chief guard) gave him two or three shots and he stopped moaning.

In fact Medvedev died before Sokolov could interview him, and so his statement is only what the White official who captured him claimed that Medvedev had said. There were other people in Ekaterinburg who came to different conclusions (Sources **F** and **G**).

Source F By Captain Malinovsky, a White officer who visited the scene in July 1918

It appeared to me that the Bolsheviks had shot someone in the room in order to simulate the murder of the imperial family.

Source G By Sir Charles Eliot, a British diplomat, who visited the scene in October 1918 and who spoke excellent Russian

On the wall and floor were the marks of seventeen bullets, but no traces of blood were visible. There is no evidence as to who the victims were but it is supposed they were five, namely the tsar, his doctor, the empress's maid and two servants. On 17 July a train with blinds down left Ekaterinburg for an unknown destination. It is the general opinion in Ekaterinburg that the empress, her son and four daughters were not murdered but were sent to the north or west.

Source **H** The bullet-ridden room

Source I Telegram from the German consul to Berlin, 10 September 1918

The Germans had a network of spies inside Russia, and they did not believe the empress was dead. On 10 September 1918 the German consul sent a telegram to his government in Berlin (Source **I**) in which he appears to know exactly where the family were.

I talked with Radek [a leading Bolshevik] again today about releasing the empress and her children. He takes the position that there is no objection in principle. I referred to the necessity of removing the imperial family from its present situation, in which it is exposed to danger from which the government is powerless to protect it. Radek promised me that he would propose this at once.

Sokolov's files also contained eyewitness reports that the royal family had been seen in the town of Perm, where the Red forces had retreated after the fall of Ekaterinburg. However, he chose not to include these in his final report. Source **J** is one of these accounts.

Questions

1 Look at Sources **C**, **G**, **I** and **J**. What evidence is there to suggest that the royal family were not all killed on 17 July?

2 Look at Source **D**. Do you think it is more or less reliable than Source **G** in trying to find out what happened to the tsar and his family? Explain your answer.

3 Does Source **E** prove that the royal family were killed at Ekaterinburg? Explain your answer.

4 Sokolov and Malinovsky were both Whites, and yet they disagree about the fate of the Russian royal family. What reasons could there be for this?

5 a) What do **you** think happened to the tsar and his family?
b) Which pieces of evidence do you think are the most important in helping you to reach your conclusion? Why do you believe them to be the most important?

One day in September I went with my brother's fiancé, Anna Kostina [Zinoviev's secretary]. The royal family were staying at the time in Berzien's rooms on Obvinskaya Street in the basement. We went down to the basement and I saw the room where in the poor candlelight I could make out the former empress Alexandra and her four daughters, who were in a terrible state, but I recognised them only too well.

Source J By Natalya Mutnykh, a nurse

It is the job of the historian to try and work out what happened by using all the evidence available. However, it is not unusual for new evidence to be discovered after the historian has reached a conclusion.

You are in exactly that position with Sources **K** and **L**. It is then the job of the historian to try and produce a new conclusion which takes into account the new evidence. It also leads the historian to look at the old evidence in a different light.

Source K A report in a British newspaper, *The Independent*, 11 December 1992

Home Office forensic scientists believe that they have solved the 74 year-old mystery surrounding the fate of the Russian royal family using a blood sample taken from the Duke of Edinburgh (the tsarina's great nephew). The scientists at Aldermaston disclosed yesterday that they had matched the Duke's blood samples with the remains of bodies believed to be those of the tsarina and her family. The tests were undertaken after nine skeletons were unearthed in a pit in Ekaterinburg in July last year. The Home Office said yesterday that DNA analysis confirmed that there was one family group among the bones and that the sexes of the bodies was consistent with identification of the remains as those of Tsar Nicholas II, Tsarina Alexandra and three of the five children.

Source L A report from a British newspaper, *The Times*, 11 December 1992

Bones from the skeletons were brought to Britain three months ago. At Aldermaston scientists began the task of extracting tiny fragments of DNA from the bones. The DNA was then sequenced. No two unrelated individuals would expect to share the same sequence. The skeletons would appear to be those of a family group and four unrelated individuals, which is consistent with accounts that suggest that the family was shot by Bolsheviks at a house in Ekaterinburg on 17 July 1918, with their doctor and three servants. Their bodies were taken away with the intention of burning them and destroying the evidence. In the event only two bodies were burnt, those of the tsar's heir, Alexei and his youngest daughter Anastasia. The rest were buried in a pit.

Questions

6 Does the evidence in Sources **K** and **L** support or contradict the evidence in Source **J**?

7 What does this tell you about the dangers of eyewitness accounts?

8 Which parts of the story given in Source **C** are supported by the evidence of Sources **K** and **L** and which parts are not?

9 Carefully read Source **L**. Which part of it is **opinion** and not **fact**?

10 What do you now believe happened to the tsar and his family? Why have you come to this conclusion?

War Communism and the New Economic Policy

Why was there famine during the civil war?
Why was the NEP so controversial?

War Communism

The policies followed by the communist government in Russia between 1918 and 1921 have become known as War Communism. The central government took control of all industry and economic activity. All factories which had more than ten workers were taken over and run by the government. The death penalty was introduced for anyone who went on strike. All private trade was banned. The aim was to keep the Red Army supplied with food and weapons so that it could win the civil war. In this respect it succeeded.

The civil war had a terrible effect on Russia. Of the ten million people who died in the civil war, over half are thought to have died from starvation.

Famine

Why was there famine in Russia during the civil war? The main reason was the policies followed by Lenin's government. They desperately needed food for the Red Army and the workers in the cities. Therefore the Cheka (see page 33) were ordered to take all spare grain from the peasants. The Cheka met with considerable opposition, and killed thousands of peasants. As a result, the peasants realised that there was no point in growing more food than they needed, since they would not be paid for any extra which they grew. This meant that much less grain was being grown by the end of the civil war. To make matters worse, there was a drought in 1920 and 1921, so the peasants' crops were poor. There was not even enough for the peasants themselves to eat, let alone a surplus for the people in the towns. The total amount of grain produced in 1921 was less than half that grown in 1913.

Source A Collecting the bodies of famine victims

Source B A Bolshevik view of the causes of the famine, written in 1919

No one can eat more than the human body can absorb. Everyone is provided for. And yet there is concealment everywhere, in the hope of selling grain to town speculators [capitalists who illegally bought grain from the peasants to sell in the cities] at fabulous prices.

Source D An eyewitness account by British refugees from Petrograd who managed to get back to London, 1918

It is a common occurrence when a horse falls down in the street for the people to cut off the flesh of the animal the moment it has breathed its last. Another way of getting food was by buying it at excessive prices from members of the Red Guard who are well fed.

Source C A letter from Lenin to Trotsky, 1 February 1918

The situation concerning railway transport is really catastrophic. Grain supplies are no longer getting through.

Crisis and protest

Famine was not the only problem faced by the Bolsheviks. Industry was also in crisis. With so little food in the cities, workers moved to the countryside where they thought there would be more food. The population of Petrograd dropped from 2.5 million in 1917 to 0.6 million in 1920. With so few workers left in the cities, industrial production collapsed.

This catastrophic situation was not what the workers and peasants had fought for. Anti-Bolshevik protests spread across the country. The most important of these was at the Kronstadt naval base near Petrograd. The sailors of Kronstadt had been loyal Bolshevik supporters throughout the revolution, even during the July days. They had been described as 'heroes of the revolution' by Trotsky.

Source E The Red Army and Fleet defend the frontiers of Russia. A Bolshevik poster from 1920 which shows the Red Army and Navy marching together in defence of the Revolution.

Questions

1 Who is blamed in Source **B** for the food shortage?

2 What other reasons for the shortage of food can you find?

3 Does this mean that Source **B** is of no use to the historian? Explain your answer.

4 Would Source **B** or Source **D** be more useful to a historian studying the famine in Russia? Give your reasons.

Source F Tukhachevsky's troops, in the distance, march across the ice to attack the Kronstadt naval base, March 1921. Most of them are wearing white sheets as camouflage.

But in March 1921, at the very moment that leading Bolsheviks from all over Russia were meeting in Petrograd for the Tenth Party Congress, the sailors of Kronstadt revolted, demanding 'Soviets without Bolsheviks'. Many workers from Petrograd crossed the frozen Neva river to join them. Trotsky now described the sailors as 'tools of tsarist generals' and White agents. While the Neva was still frozen he ordered General Tukhachevsky to storm the base with 60 000 Red Army troops. After fierce fighting the Kronstadt rebels were defeated and the leaders shot.

Lenin had feared that if the Kronstadt sailors had been successful in their protests, it would have encouraged workers all over Russia to rebel and the Bolsheviks would have been unable to cope. The crushing of the Kronstadt revolt showed just how ruthless Lenin could be. However, at this point he once more displayed the ability to change his policy to meet new circumstances, an ability that enabled the Bolsheviks to overcome so many problems. Lenin decided to abandon the policy of War Communism, which had caused the revolt, and he replaced it with the New Economic Policy.

The New Economic Policy

Lenin introduced the New Economic Policy (NEP) in March 1921. He was aware that War Communism had failed because the peasants had no incentive to grow more food. The NEP dealt with this problem in two ways:

- Peasants were to be allowed to sell any surplus food which they produced. This meant that the more food they grew, the more money they could earn.
- However, this would not work unless there were goods for them to buy. Therefore, factories which had fewer than 20 workers were to be given back to their owners.

Some Bolsheviks, such as Trotsky, were not happy with the NEP. They felt that the state control of War Communism was the correct way to produce a communist society. However, Lenin, as ever, was a realist. Unlike Trotsky, he was willing to abandon a strictly Marxist approach in order to remain in power.

Lenin believed that unless the standard of living of the people improved, the Bolsheviks would lose power, and if the Bolsheviks lost power then the Revolution would be over.

Source G Lenin on the introduction of the NEP

Some people sneer 'See what communism has come to, it is like a man on crutches'. I have heard enough of insults of this kind. Russia emerged from seven years of war in a state that can most of all be likened to that of a man beaten to within an inch of his life. To think that we can get out of this state without crutches is to understand nothing.

So the NEP was to be the crutch to allow Russia to recover from the crisis. To those of his critics who accused him of reintroducing the hated capitalist system, he replied:

'Let the peasants have their little bit of capitalism, as long as we keep power. The Proletarian government is in no danger as long as it firmly holds transport and large-scale industry in its hands.'

Lenin referred to these as 'the commanding heights of industry'.

The story of the NEP is not one of complete success. Certainly agricultural production recovered quickly. The peasants were willing to grow more food now they could make a profit by selling their surplus produce, and the good weather of 1922 and 1923 led to much better harvests. However with so much more being grown the price of food naturally dropped.

In contrast, industry did not recover at the same speed. The workers who had fled the cities in search of land and food did not quickly return. Therefore, factories could not produce enough and so there were shortages of many goods. This led to the price of these goods going up. In other words, the price of industrial goods was going up at the same time as agricultural prices were going down. Trotsky called this the 'scissors crisis', because the gap between agricultural and industrial prices was widening like an opening pair of scissors.

It was a serious crisis because there would soon be no reason for the peasants to grow surplus food, since they would not be able to afford any industrial goods. Russia would then slide back into the terrible famine from which she had only just recovered.

Source H The Russian grain harvest, 1913–25 (in millions of tonnes)

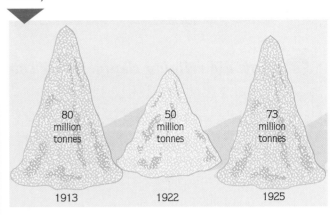

Source I Russian coal production, 1913–25 (in millions of tonnes)

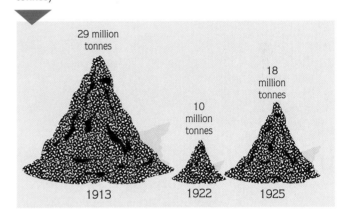

Trotsky and his supporters believed the scissors crisis proved that the NEP was a disaster, since it reintroduced capitalism but did not make sure that the peasants grew enough food to supply the rest of Russia. However, after October 1923 the blades of the 'scissors' began to close as industrial production continued to grow and prices fell as a result.

Questions

1 Look at Sources **H** and **I** and the text on these pages.
   a) What do they tell you about grain and coal production?
   b) Do they suggest that the NEP was a success?

2 Why did some communists believe that the NEP was a failure?

3 **a)** Look at Source **G**. What was Lenin's view of the NEP?
   b) How would he have judged whether the NEP was a success or not?

4 Life under the communists

Religion under communism

 How did religion change under communism?

The Orthodox Church

Since the fifteenth century the Russian Orthodox Church had been independent of all other Christian Churches. The people of Russia regarded their country as more favoured by God than any other country, and referred to it as Holy Russia. As the ruler of Russia, the tsar was therefore regarded as a very special ruler indeed. The Orthodox Church taught that it was the duty of all Russians to obey the tsar.

While the bishops and leaders of the Orthodox Church were educated and respected men, the situation in the villages was very different. Village priests were usually poorly educated. They were poorly paid and lived like peasants. They grew long hair and beards to imitate the way Christ was supposed to have looked. Some villages might also contain a starets, or holy man, who was often a monk. A starets was

greatly respected by the people, who would come to him with their problems. When a starets died, they were often declared to be saints, and their bodies displayed in glass cases in the local church. However not all starets led holy lives, as the example of Rasputin shows (see page 25).

Religious ceremonies were very important events in the lives of the peasants. Source **A** shows a whole village in procession behind a religious relic which is being carried by a group of monks.

Pogroms

Under the rule of Tsar Nicholas II, the Easter festivals were often used to hold pogroms – attacks against the Jews. During a pogrom, mobs would break into the

Jewish parts of towns to loot, rape and sometimes kill the inhabitants. Pogroms had occurred before the reign of Nicholas II and previous tsars had introduced laws which restricted where Jews could live. However, Nicholas encouraged a much more brutal approach, and was probably a member of the Black Hundred, a group formed to organise anti-Semitic (anti-Jewish) propaganda and pogroms.

The tsar's attitude to Jews can be shown by his treatment of wounded Jewish soldiers who returned from fighting in the Russian army against Japan in 1905. Many of them had their land taken from them because it was claimed they had left the area set aside for Jews to live in!

The Church under the communists

When Lenin and the Bolsheviks came to power the Church presented them with a problem. While the new government was atheist (did not believe in any god), the vast majority of Russians were deeply religious. Karl Marx had described religion as 'the opiate of the people' – that is, a drug which kept them content so that they did not rebel against their oppression. However, Lenin was more concerned that if he left it alone, the Orthodox Church would become a centre of organised resistance to communism. He dealt with this situation by allowing the people freedom of belief and worship, while destroying the power and wealth of the Church. All church property was seized by the state and the clergy were made to pay high taxes.

As the Church was so closely associated with the tsar and his autocratic rule, these measures were probably not unpopular with many people. During the famine of 1922 some priests were killed when they refused to hand over church valuables to help pay for famine relief. Although the local church might be closed and the local priest in prison, Lenin allowed people to continue their personal religious beliefs and still belong to the Communist Party.

This once again shows Lenin's ability to act according to the circumstances. There were simply too many religious people in Russia for the communists to be able to destroy religion completely. However, religious instruction was banned in schools, as Lenin hoped that with time religion would die out.

Source B Grain being stored in a disused church

Source C Anti-Jewish poster issued by Stalin (see page 57) showing Trotsky as a Jew responsible for the death of Russians

Questions

1 Look at Source **A**. Find examples to show:
   a) the poverty of the peasantry,
   b) the importance of religion for the people,
   c) the brutality of the tsarist police.

2 Look at Sources **A**, **B** and **C** and the text.
   In what ways had religion changed under the communists and in what ways had it stayed the same? When you answer this question consider the following:
   a) the power and wealth of the Church,
   b) people's beliefs,
   c) anti-Semitism.

Art under Nicholas II and Lenin

In what ways did art change under the communists?
Why did these changes happen?

Realism

During the second half of the nineteenth century the arts in Russia were dominated by a very realistic style which accurately portrayed the lives of ordinary Russian people.

In Source **A** the artist, Repin shows very truthfully what a hard life the boatmen had, pulling the boats along the river. Another of Repin's paintings is shown on page 48. According to Repin, in his paintings he was trying to 'criticise all the monstrosities of our terrible society'. This realism was also evident in the work of the great Russian novelist Leo Tolstoy, who hoped to improve the lives of the poor by revealing the horror of their lives to the powerful people who read his books.

World of Art

At the end of the nineteenth century there emerged a new artistic movement in Russia which rejected this detailed realism. They took their inspiration from the French impressionist painters of the time, and the new more decorative Art Nouveau style which was then popular all over Europe. These Russian artists did not believe that it was their task to portray simply what could be seen on the surface, but rather they sought to show an inner truth.

They were known as the World of Art group, and their activities were organised by Sergei Diaghilev. He published their work in a magazine which gave its name to the movement and he also put on exhibitions of their work. The World of Art movement was not limited to painting. Diaghilev also founded the Ballets Russes (Russian Ballet) which was based in Paris. The Ballets Russes used Russian artists to design sets and costumes for their dreamlike ballets, with music by modern Russian composers such as Stravinsky, and performed by Russian dancers such as Nijinsky.

Source A The Volga Boatmen by Ilya Repin, painted between 1870 and 1873

Source B *Spring* by Victor Borisov-Musatov, painted in 1898. He was one of the most popular of the World of Art artists. This picture, like so many of his works, shows a perfect fantasy world.

Source C Costume for the Ballets Russes production of Stravinsky's ballet *The Firebird*, which was based on an old Russian folk story.

Source D The 1899 Easter egg for the tsarina by Fabergé. The enamel egg is decorated in gold and diamonds. It is a clock, with the central band revolving to tell the time.

The work of the World of Art artists was very popular with the rich people of Russia. Whereas very few middle-class people had bought large numbers of realist paintings, many merchants and nobles bought examples of the new art. However, after the October Revolution many rich Russians fled to other countries as the Bolsheviks tried to take their wealth from them. The Bolsheviks had little use for this new style of art, and so many of the artists went into exile abroad.

The Avant-garde

The creative explosion in Russia did not end with the World of Art, but developed further with the avant-garde artists. Whereas the Realists and the World of Art group relied on the rich to buy their work, and so had to create work to please their customers, the avant-garde artists saw themselves as revolutionaries, overturning existing ideas about art. They were trying to produce a completely new style of art for a new era – the twentieth century – by stripping art to its bare essentials.

A similar exotic approach was displayed by the jeweller Fabergé. From 1881 onwards he was commissioned by Tsar Nicholas II to produce two jewelled eggs each Easter as presents for his mother and his wife. Nicholas was also a subscriber to the *World of Art* magazine.

Source E Haymaking by Kazimir Malevich, painted in 1909. Malevich finally declared that painting was dead after reducing his pictures to white squares on a white background.

Lenin and art

The avant-garde artists already saw themselves as revolutionaries, and so many of them joined the Bolsheviks, especially after the success of the October Revolution. They produced posters supporting the Bolsheviks, for example Lissitsky's *Red Wedge* (see page 38). The new Bolshevik government set up a special department for art, and this was dominated by avant-garde artists such as Kazimir Malevich and Vassili Kandinski.

For a while, Russia became the leading country for avant-garde artistic experiment. Many of these artists wished to destroy all the art of the past, as they were concerned only with the future. However, Lenin did not agree with them. He said 'we must preserve the beautiful, even if it is old'. Lenin ordered the government to take control of the art collections which had once belonged to the rich merchants. More importantly, they also took over the Tretyakov Gallery, which was full of nineteenth-century realist paintings.

Lenin had no use for avant-garde art because it was neither loved nor understood by the people. Lenin much preferred a group of artists who were known as the Association of Artists of Revolutionary Russia. They said 'We will depict the life of the Red Army, the workers, the peasants and the heroes of labour'. This heroic realism, which was later known as 'Socialist Realism', was exactly what Lenin had in mind. It was the duty of art to make sure that the message of the revolution was understood by everyone.

As the realist artists were so popular with the leading Bolsheviks, there was little work for the avant-garde artists. Some avant-garde artists decided to leave Russia and go to Western Europe, while others like Malevich turned to architecture.

Source F
Lenin's views on art

Art belongs to the people. It should be understood and loved by these people. It should bring together the thought and will of these people and elevate them.

Source G Lenin's speech to the workers at the Putilov factory in May 1917, painted by Brodski in 1929. It is in the realist style preferred by Lenin. It gives the impression that in May 1917 all of the workers were united behind a single leader – Lenin.

1 What evidence is there to suggest that the work of the World of Art group was popular with the rich people of Russia?

2 What differences are there between Source **B** and Source **A**?

3 As supporters of the Bolsheviks, the avant-garde artists expected to dominate art after the communist Revolution in 1917. Why did this not happen?

4 Look at Sources **A** and **G**.
a) What is similar about the style and content of these two paintings?
b) What is different about the content of the two paintings?
c) What is different about the purpose of the two paintings?

Questions

Poster art

In an age before the invention of television and radio, the most effective way of advertising was coloured posters stuck on walls and windows. In the early years of the twentieth century they were very popular with Russian companies who used them to try and sell their products.

With the success of the Bolshevik Revolution, everything changed. Posters were no longer to sell household products – their purpose was now to get the Bolshevik message across to every corner of the huge Russian Empire. In a state where many people were unable to read and write a simple poster like Source **I** could get across a message to far more people than a newspaper.

Pravda, the Bolshevik newspaper, claimed that they produced 375 000 posters in 1919 alone. Many posters contained the notice 'Anybody who tears down or covers this poster is committing a counter-revolutionary act'.

Poster artists became heroes of the revolution, as is shown by Source **J**.

Working tirelessly for the Military Department since the beginning of 1919, Comrade Moor has given great service to the Red Army with his bold poster designs. During the past three years Comrade Moor has designed 150 posters for the Red Army. The Military Revolutionary Committee of the Republic honours him for the heroic battle he has fought with his own particular weapons – the brush and pencil.

Questions

1 Why did the Bolsheviks regard posters as so important?

2 How did posters change under the Bolsheviks? Why did this happen?

3 The Treaty of Brest-Litovsk has just been signed. Draw a Bolshevik poster of your own which supports the treaty.

4 What changes occurred to art in Russia between the late nineteenth century and 1924? What caused these changes?

Women and the Revolution

How did the communist Revolution change the lives of women in Russia?

Living conditions before the Revolution

Peasant women lived a very difficult life, treated almost as property and exhausted by childbirth and hard work in the fields. With the industrialisation which took place in the final decades of tsarist Russia, women as well as men moved to the cities for work. For them, life there was even more difficult. Not only did they have to work long hours, but often they were only paid half as much as men. There was no time off work for pregnancy and thousands of babies died of malnutrition.

For most women the choice was either to leave the baby with a minder or send it back to the home village where it would be better looked after but the mother would rarely get the chance to see it.

It was hardly surprising that women were involved in many of the strikes which broke out at this time. For example in 1895 1500 women at the St. Petersburg Laferme cigarette factory went on strike and smashed equipment in the factory.

Women's movements

During the 1905 revolution a group of wealthy St. Petersburg women formed the Union of Women's Equality to campaign for women's right to vote. Women members of the Bolsheviks, notably Alexandra Kollontai, attended the first meeting. They declared their opposition on the ground that wealthy women had nothing in common with working-class women. Women could not hope to gain equality, they said, until the Revolution had removed the difference between rich and poor.

The Duma ignored the demands of the Union of Women's Equality. Kollontai found it difficult to get many of the Bolshevik men to take women's issues seriously. Men in the Bolshevik Party believed that equality would automatically happen once the Revolution took place, and therefore working for the Revolution was all that mattered.

Women and the First World War

With millions of men fighting in the war there was a shortage of workers. Jobs which had once been done by men only were taken over by women, such as bus drivers and conductors. This did not mean that life became any easier for many women. Prices shot up and food was in short supply (see page 24). With the men away, many women were bringing up a family on their own.

When the sale of bread was suspended in Moscow in April 1915, women broke into bread shops and looted them. Many women wanted an end to the war, and the Bolsheviks were the only party who supported this. The most important protest came on 23 February 1917, International Women's Day. The meeting of international socialist parties in 1910 had decided to make 8 March (23 February in Russia – remember, they used a different calender – see page 24), International Women's Day, to be celebrated by socialists throughout the world. Women joined the workers from the Putilov works. There were as many as 200 000 people on the streets of Petrograd. This protest turned into the general strike which helped to bring tsarism to an end.

After the Revolution

Lenin was more sympathetic to the demands of women than were many other Bolsheviks. He set up a women's commission under the leadership of his friend Inessa Armand. Its job was to discover the needs of women so that a programme of reforms could be drawn up. Lenin then set up a women's department of Sovnarkom (see page 33) – called Zhenotdel. Alexandra Kollontai became its head – the first woman ever to be a member of a European government. As a result, the following laws were passed:

- A new marriage law was passed in December 1917 making it legal for men over 18 and women over 16 to marry;
- Divorce became available simply by one partner in the marriage asking for it;
- In 1920 abortion on demand was made legal in all state hospitals. Before, many women had died or been seriously injured in back-street operations.

However, the civil war and War Communism still meant that there were terrible food shortages, and that women were still bringing up children on their own.

The Stalinist era

Stalin was far less sympathetic to the women's movement, and in 1930 he abolished Zhenotdel.

In the late 1920s there was a significant fall in the birth rate, and Stalin's industrialisation required an ever-increasing work force, not a smaller one. Therefore he made it much more expensive to get a divorce, and made abortion available only where the mother's health was threatened. Special tax benefits were given to people with large families and extra taxes were placed on unmarried people and childless couples. In 1944 a new honour of 'Mother-Heroine' was created for all women who produced 10 children.

Under communism, women still found equality difficult to achieve. Industrialisation required a huge increase in the number of workers, and many of these were women. With easier divorces allowed in the 1920s, more and more women found themselves bringing up families on their own. Therefore they were not only having to do the same job as men during the day, but bring up a family as well.

While factory jobs were easily available, it was far more difficult for a woman to get a senior post. Even in 1957 only 4 of the 175 members of the Party Central Committee were women. Some careers were open to women. In 1913 there had been only 23 000 doctors in the whole of Russia and just 10 per cent of those had been women. By 1940 there were 155 000 doctors, over half of whom were women.

Source B A woman worker in a Russian turbine factory in 1936

Source C A Russian government poster from 1931, showing women and men doing the same jobs in a factory

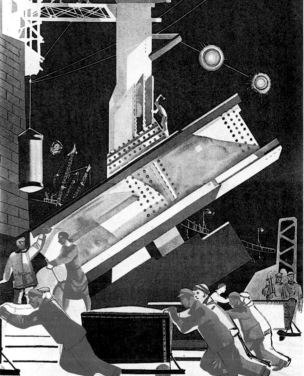

Questions

1 Sources **B** and **C** show women doing the same jobs as men. Were women treated as equal to men under communism? Explain your answer.

2 In 1918 Alexandra Kollontai said 'The revolution has brought rights for women on paper, but in fact it has made life harder for them'.
   a) What did she mean by 'rights on paper'?
   b) Do you think that she would have made the same statement in 1940, after 23 years of communist government? Explain your answer.

Source A A photograph of Lenin taken during his final illness

Source B The four candidates

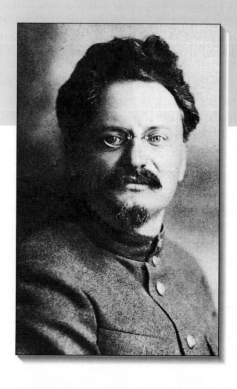

S T R E N G T H S	Trotsky
	• Key figure in organising the October Revolution.
	• Creator of the Red Army and hero of the victory in the civil war.
	• Regarded by Lenin as the 'ablest man in the Central Committee'.

W E A K N E S S E S	
	• A former Menshevik. Trotsky only joined the Bolsheviks in late summer 1917. Therefore distrusted by those who had been in the Bolshevik Party for many years.
	• A Jew. When Lenin had suggested to Trotsky that he was the best man to take over from Lenin, Trotsky had replied that there were too many Bolsheviks who hated Jews.

The possible successors to Lenin

From late 1921 until his death in January 1924 Lenin suffered a series of strokes, the third of which, in March 1923, left him permanently speechless. Despite his power, Lenin had never ordered the other leading Bolsheviks to obey him. He had always relied on persuading them that he was right. Now he had lost that power of persuasion. During Lenin's final illness the USSR was ruled by Stalin, Kamenev and Zinoviev. These three, along with Trotsky, were the men most likely to succeed Lenin as the new communist leader.

Lenin's Testament

After Lenin died, his body was brought to Moscow where it was embalmed and put in a glass case, just like a saint of the Russian Orthodox Church. In December 1922, Lenin had dictated his Testament (Source **C**), in which he summed up his opinion of the leaders of the party. At this time, Stalin had greatly angered him and insulted Krupskaya, Lenin's wife. In January 1923 Lenin had added a postscript on Stalin. After Lenin's death, Krupskaya insisted that the Testament be published by the Party Central Committee. In May 1924 the Central Committee discussed the Testament but decided not to publish it.

Kamenev	Zinoviev	Stalin
• Long-standing member of the Bolsheviks and close associate of Lenin.	• Founder member of the Bolshevik Party. • Worked closely with Lenin between 1903 and 1917.	• Long-standing member of the Bolshevik Party, though not a senior member until after 1912. • A member of Sovnarcom. • General Secretary of the Communist Party from 1922 onwards. This gave him the power to promote and dismiss people from important jobs within the party, and to set the agenda for Politburo meetings. • A peasant, and not a member of the bourgeoisie like the other leading Bolsheviks. Therefore popular with many rank-and-file members.
• Had greatly angered Lenin and many other Bolsheviks by openly opposing the October Revolution. Therefore had not been given a post in the 1917 Sovnarcom (see page 33). • A Jew (see comment on Trotsky).	• As with Kamenev, openly opposed the October Revolution and so also not given a post in Sovnarcom. • A Jew (see comment on Trotsky).	• Lost Lenin's support at the end of Lenin's life.

Since he has become General Secretary, Comrade Stalin has concentrated enormous power in his hands and I am not sure that he will always know how to use that power with caution. On the other hand, Comrade Trotsky is the most capable man in the present Central Committee, but he is also too self-confident.

I will simply remind you that the October 1917 episode involving Zinoviev and Kamenev was not accidental but that it ought not to be used against them, any more than the non-Bolshevism of Trotsky.

Postscript

Stalin is too rude, and this fault is insupportable in a General Secretary. Therefore I propose to the comrades to find a way to remove Stalin from that position and to appoint to it another man who will be more patient, more loyal, more polite, less unpredictable and more considerate to his comrades.

Source D   Montage photograph of Lenin and Stalin. A photograph of Stalin has been placed next to Lenin to make it look as though they were photographed sitting together.

Lenin's funeral

All the communist leaders except Trotsky were present at Lenin's funeral. Trotsky was suffering from malaria and was on a train heading for the warmer climate of the south. He later claimed that Stalin had lied to him about the date of the funeral so that Trotsky had thought he did not have enough time to return to Moscow.

Whether this was true or not, Trotsky's absence was a serious mistake, as it looked as though he was insulting Lenin, at the very moment when the party were treating Lenin like a saint. Indeed, it was decided to preserve Lenin's body and display it in a mausoleum in the centre of Moscow. As with the failure to press for publication of Lenin's Testament, it was a serious miscalculation by Trotsky not to attend the funeral.

Socialism in One Country

The struggle for power was not fought on a personal basis, but over policy. Stalin, Kamenev and Zinoviev attacked Trotsky over his policy of permanent world revolution. Trotsky maintained that the USSR could not survive against the hostile powers of Europe. He believed, therefore, that the communists must export revolution to the rest of the world, so that there would be a revolution in every country. Furthermore the communists should build up Russian industry as quickly as possible, so that a revolutionary proletariat could develop in Russia.

These were old Menshevik policies and the other three attacked them as such. They maintained that the theory of permanent revolution was at odds with the New Economic Policy, which sought to help the revolution survive in Russia. They proposed a new policy – Socialism in One Country. World revolution was to be abandoned for the time being and the communists would concentrate on building a modern, industrial state, strong enough to defend itself from hostile countries. At the 13th Party Congress of 1924, Trotsky was defeated and he accepted this defeat, since he supported the idea of a united party.

Once Trotsky was defeated, Stalin adopted his policy of rapid industrialisation, and used it to attack Zinoviev and Kamenev, who continued to oppose it. The 14th Party Congress of 1925 supported the new industrial policy and Zinoviev and Kamenev were defeated. Using his position as General Secretary, Stalin had hand-picked many of the delegates so that his victory was guaranteed. In 1925 Trotsky was sacked as Commissar of War, and the following year Zinoviev and Kamenev were sacked from the Politburo. Finally, in 1927, Trotsky was expelled from the party.

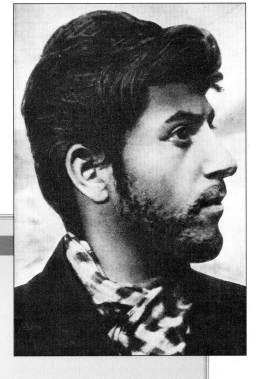

Source E Lenin's funeral. Thousands stand in the snow while Lenin's body is taken to the tomb. An eyewitness, Nadezhda Mandelstam, described it as 'like the funeral of a tsar'. Petrograd was renamed Leningrad in his honour.

Stalin

Stalin was born Josef Djugashvili. Unlike most of the other Bolshevik leaders, his parents were not bourgeoisie and they were not Russian. Stalin was a peasant from Georgia, a republic in the east of the Soviet Union. He was the star pupil at his local school and he won a scholarship to train as a priest. At the college he joined the Social Democrats and supported Lenin when the Bolsheviks broke away. At first he took the name of Koba but later changed this to Stalin, which meant 'Man of Steel'.

During 1917 Stalin was editor of *Pravda*, the party newspaper, and then Lenin appointed him Commissar of Nationalities in the Bolshevik government. As a Georgian, he perhaps seemed the obvious choice to stop the non-Russian people in the empire from declaring independence from Russia. Remember that the tsar's empire had been made up of 22 different nationalities. They had resented Russian rule, and feared the same domination under the communists.

Stalin ordered the Red Army to invade Georgia when it wanted to become independent from Russia, and it was this that led Lenin to write the postscript to his Testament.

Questions

1 Which leader would have suffered most if Lenin's Testament had been published?

2 Why do you think that the leadership of the Communist Party all agreed that it should not be published?

3 What point was being made in Source **D**?

4 Does Source **C** support Source **D**? Explain your answer.

5 Why do you think Stalin was able to defeat his rivals in the struggle for power?

You should consider:
- Stalin's position as General Secretary of the Communist Party,
- Trotsky's mistakes,
- Kamenev and Zinoviev's mistakes,
- Stalin's policies.

6 Which one of the four causes in Question 5 do you think is the most important to explain why Stalin gained power? Look at each of the other three in turn, and decide how they would have been affected if the one you have chosen had not occurred.

Collectivisation

**Why did Stalin force the rapid collectivisation of agriculture?
How did collectivisation affect Russia?**

The problem

Stalin had decided on rapid industrialisation. The problem was how to finance it. Western nations would not invest in a communist country. The solution was to sell Russian agricultural produce abroad to earn enough to buy industrial machinery. This meant that Russian agriculture needed to produce much more, as industrialisation meant more peasants leaving the land to work in the factories. There would be more Russians to feed who would no longer be growing their own food.

However, Russian agriculture was in no position to produce so much more food. This would require large efficient farms and modern machinery. After the Revolution, the communists won the support of the peasants by allowing them to seize the land of the rich landowners and divide it among themselves. This meant that the average farm was smaller than it had been before the First World War. Although the New Economic Policy had encouraged peasants to produce more food, the grain harvest had still not recovered to the level of 1913, let alone the level necessary for Stalin's plans.

The solution

Stalin's solution was to encourage peasants to join collective farms, where groups of peasants would give up the right to own land in return for sharing the produce of the collective. Such farms would be large enough to own modern machinery. It was planned that by 1933 20 per cent of all farmland would be farmed by collectives.

While Source **B** suggests that Stalin was going to use peaceful methods, Source **C** shows the reality was very different. While peasants who did not own any land might find collectives attractive, most peasants did not want to lose the land which they had gained after the Revolution. Stalin responded by launching all out warfare on the richer peasants or kulaks.

A force of 25 000 workers, the first of many, were sent into the countryside to 'encourage' the peasants to join the collectives. Kulak families were thrown off their land, which was then given to the collectives.

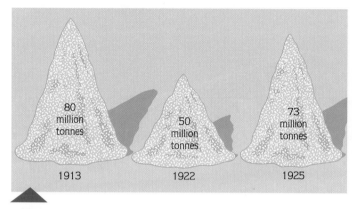

Source A   The grain harvest in Russia 1913–25

Source B   Stalin addressing the party conference in 1927

What is the way out? The way out is to turn the small and scattered peasant farms into large, united farms based on the cultivation of land in common...not by pressure, but by example and persuasion.

Source C   Stalin addressing the party conference in 1929

We must smash the kulaks...we must strike at the kulaks so hard as to prevent them rising to their feet again. We must destroy them as a social class.

Many kulak families were deported to distant regions of the country. It is impossible to find an accurate figure, but possibly as many as ten million people were deported in the war against the kulaks. Even those peasants who were not deported saw no point in handing over their animals to the collectives. Therefore they killed and ate them. The scale of the slaughter was staggering. From a total of 60 million cows 30 million were killed, while 16 million horses died from a total of 34 million. The novelist Sholokhov describes a typical scene in Source **D**.

Source D From *Virgin Soil Upturned*, a novel by Sholokhov written in 1934. Sholokhov was living in Russia during collectivisation.

Both those who had joined the Kolkhoz [collective] and individual farmers killed their stock. Bulls, sheep, pigs, even cows were slaughtered. The dogs began to drag entrails around the village; cellars and barns were full of meat…Young and old suffered from stomachache. At dinner times tables groaned under boiled and roasted meat.

Stalin's response was to do what Lenin had done during the civil war. Squads of men were sent out into the countryside to seize grain and the peasants were left to starve. Of course the government kept no accurate figures, but between six and ten million peasants probably died during the famine of 1932–3. However, Stalin got his way. By 1932, 61.5 per cent of all peasants were living in collectives, three times as many as originally planned. By 1936 89.6 per cent of peasants were on collective farms.

Source G A party worker explaining about collectivisation to the peasants

Source E The grain harvest in Russia 1930–32

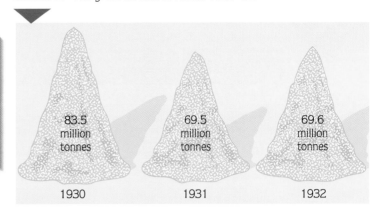

Source F Russian grain exports 1929–32

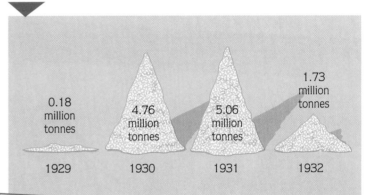

Source H
A collective farm work team, painted by Alexandre Deineka in 1934

Questions

1 What were the aims of collectivisation?

2 Compare Sources **A**, **E** and **F**. Did collectivisation achieve its aim? Give evidence from these sources.

3 In a conversation with Winston Churchill, the British prime minister, Stalin described collectivisation as 'terrible but necessary'.
   a) In what ways was it terrible?
   b) In what ways could Stalin argue that it had been a success?

3 **a)** What view of collectivisation is shown by Sources **G** and **H**?

b) In what ways do they conflict with the evidence of the peasants' attitude to collective farms?
c) Source **G** is a photograph whereas Source **H** is a painting. Does this mean that **G** is more reliable than **H**? Give your reasons.

4 Source **D** is from a novel. Does this mean it is of no use to the historian? Give reasons for your answer.

5 What problems does the historian face when trying to build up an accurate picture of what happened during the process of collectivisation?
   Look in particular at the nature of the evidence in this chapter.

Industrialisation

▶ *Why did Stalin want to industrialise the Soviet Union?*
What were the effects of industrialisation?

The survival of communism

Lenin had seen technology as vital to communism. He wanted to be able to convince everyone of the benefits of communism, and technology was to be one way of doing this. Lenin hoped to bring electricity into every home for people to see that communism led to a better life (Source **A**).

Stalin had very different aims when he decided to speed up the development of industry. As we saw on page 58, Stalin adopted Trotsky's argument that industrialisation was necessary to build up a revolutionary proletariat. However, to this he added a new argument, adapting industrialisation to the new policy of Socialism in One Country.

Stalin believed that the already industrialised capitalist countries of the world were preparing to destroy Soviet Russia, and so Russia must build up her industry to their level within ten years, to ensure that the Russian army would be well enough equipped to repel the capitalist forces. Stalin turned industrialisation into a heroic crusade to ensure the survival of communism.

Source A Leninist poster – 'Communism is soviet power plus the electrification of the whole country'

Source B Speech by Stalin in 1931

If you are backward and weak then you...may be beaten and enslaved. But if you are powerful... people must beware of you. We are fifty to one hundred years behind the advanced countries. We must make up this gap in ten years. Either we do this or they crush us.

Source C *Higher and higher* by Serafima Ryangina, 1934. This propaganda painting expressed industrialisation as a crusade. It is summed up by Stalin's phrase 'There is no fortress that we Bolsheviks cannot storm'.

The Five Year Plans

In 1928 a series of target production figures were set for Soviet industry to reach by 1933. Very high targets were set for iron and steel as well as oil, since these would be crucial to the development of the armed forces. By contrast, very little importance was placed on consumer goods. It was not the aim of industrialisation to raise the living standards of the workers. They had to sacrifice such things for the good of the state. Electricity was developed with the building of huge hydro-electric plants on the many major rivers of Russia, but its main purpose was to power factories, not homes.

Stalin declared that the first Five Year Plan had met its targets a year early (see Source **D**), and so a new Five Year Plan was begun. This ran the full five years, while the third Five Year Plan was brought to a sudden end by the German invasion of Russia in 1941.

In 1921 Lenin had set up GOSPLAN, the State Planning Commission, to provide guidelines of how much industry and agriculture could produce. Stalin now changed the role of the commission, so that it now set targets for every factory in every industry.

How accurate are the figures?

The last column of Source **D** shows the estimated production figures for 1932. The official Russian figures show production much higher, but these are very inaccurate. This is because many of the targets were unrealistic, but local factory managers would be punished and branded as enemies of socialism if the targets were not met. Therefore they would send in false figures rather than risk being sent with their families to labour camps or mines in Siberia.

Industry	1927-8 production	Target for 1932	1932 production
Electricity(milliard kWh)	5.05	17.0	13.4
Coal (million tonnes)	35.4	68.0	64.3
Oil (million tonnes)	11.7	19.0	21.4
Steel (million tonnes)	4.0	8.3	5.9
All textiles	5 834 000 (43%)	24 391 000 (59%)	32 715 000 (71%)
Cottons	797 000 (6%)	16 339 000 (40%)	22 398 000 (48%)
Woollens	3 882 000 (29%)	6 800 000 (16%)	7 321 000 (16%)

Source D The First Five Year Plan

Questions

1 Look at Source A. Why did Lenin want to develop electricity in Russia?

2 What were the differences between Lenin's and Stalin's views of industrialisation?

Working conditions

As industry expanded it needed a much larger workforce. This mainly consisted of unskilled peasants from the countryside.

Stalin did not concern himself with the quality of what was being produced. For him, quantity was everything. Millions of young workers belonged to 'shock brigades', who competed with one another to increase their output. They would work on their rest days and never be late. They put pressure on other workers to work harder. Stalin also allowed some people to earn far more than others if they worked harder. He used higher wages to encourage greater production.

Source E A poster from around 1930 which was hung on factory walls, and on which the names of 'slackers and doubters' could be written by their fellow workers

Life was hard for workers. A seven-day working week was introduced so that factories never stopped production. Absenteeism or being late for work became crimes against the state. Accidentally damaging tools was treated as 'sabotage'. For this workers could be sacked and so lose the housing provided by the factory. While many new factories were built, far less was spent on building houses for workers. Therefore, there was terrible overcrowding in the cities, with flats often having a family in each room.

Beyond the Urals

Virtually all Russian industry had previously been located to the west of the Ural Mountains. By locating new industry in Siberia and the east of the Soviet Union, Stalin was ensuring that Russian industry would survive an invasion from Western Europe.

Stakhanov

Alexei Stakhanov became a hero because, on the night of 30–31 August 1935, it was claimed he had shifted 102 tonnes of coal, almost 15 times the normal amount for a single shift. Other workers were encouraged to follow Stakhanov's example and were rewarded with medals, new houses and other benefits. However, the campaign was quietly dropped in the late 1930s after a number of these 'Stakhanovites' were beaten up and killed by their fellow workers.

Stakhanov in heroic pose

Huge new industrial centres such as Magnitogorsk were built. These new centres were built despite the shortage of modern equipment (Source **F**). Workers often lived in tents, and many died in the Siberian winters. However, as these cities grew, they provided a standard of living previously unknown to Russian workers. An English visitor to Magnitogorsk in the early 1930s reported that it had 'ten theatres with a total seating capacity of 9000, all attached to clubs with drama classes, chess, art and reading groups'.

Source F By John Scott, an American communist and eyewitness

Magnitogorsk was built from scratch. This was done without sufficient labour, without necessary quantities of the most elementary materials. Brigades of young enthusiasts from every corner of the Soviet Union arrived in the summer of 1930 and did the groundwork of railroad and dam construction. Later, groups of peasants came to Magnitogorsk because of the bad conditions in the villages, due to collectivisation. From 1928 until 1932 nearly a quarter of a million people came to Magnitogorsk. About three quarters of these new arrivals came of their own free will. The rest came under compulsion.

The Gulag

Industrialisation required an enormous amount of labour. People accused of being kulaks or industrial saboteurs were sent to the new labour camps. The first major project using this slave labour was the Belomor Canal, a 500 km canal linking the White Sea to the Baltic Sea. Nearly 300 000 prisoners, or zeks, worked on this canal. Even without machinery, they completed it in just twenty months, despite the conditions described in Source **H**. As many as 100 000 zeks may have died building the canal.

Source H A photograph showing the conditions during the building of the Belomor Canal. Only hand tools, such as picks and shovels, were used.

Source J Comparative production figures for Russia, the USA and Germany in 1913 and 1940

1913 Country	Pig iron (million tonnes)	Steel (million tonnes)	Coal (million tonnes)
Russia	4.8	5.2	36.5
USA	31.3	31.8	518.0
UK	10.4	7.8	291.0
Germany	19.6	18.5	193.0
France	5.2	4.8	41.4

1940 Country	Pig iron (million tonnes)	Steel (million tonnes)	Coal (million tonnes)
Russia	15.1	18.6	167.2
USA	32.4	47.9	364.7
UK	6.8	10.4	230.6
Germany	18.5	23.0	188.9
France	6.0	6.1	46.2

Source G An eyewitness account of conditions during the building of the Belomor Canal

At the end of the day there were corpses left on the work site...Two were frozen back to back leaning against each other...At night sledges went out and collected them...In the summer, bones remained from corpses which had not been removed in time, and together with the shingle they got into the concrete of the last lock at the city of Belomorsk and will be preserved there forever.

By 1939 the number of people working in labour camps may have reached as many as 12 million (see page 68). Conditions in the camps were so bad that the zeks did not usually live for more than two years.

Was Russian industrialisation a success?

Go back to the start of this unit to remind yourself of the aims of industrialisation, and then look at Sources **F** and **G**. This will help you decide whether or not industrialisation in Russia achieved its aims. Remember that Russian economic growth took place when western countries were undergoing the Great Depression, with millions of people out of work.

Source I By A. Ulam, a modern historian

Industrialisation was cruel in its effects on millions of human beings, but still it laid the foundations for a richer economy, enabling Russia to withstand a foreign invasion and become a superpower.

Questions

1 Look at Source **F**.
   a) Who do you think Scott is referring to when he says that three quarters of the workers came of their own free will? Do you think it was really a free choice for all of them?
   b) Who were those who were compelled to go to Magnitogorsk?

2 Look at Source **E**. What does this tell you about life in Russian factories at this time?

3 What changes took place in Russia as a result of industrialisation? Divide your answer into two parts:
   a) Those changes which made life better for Russians.
   b) Those changes that made life worse.

4 'Change and progress are exactly the same'. Using examples from this unit, explain whether you agree or disagree with this statement.

Terror

▶ ***What effect did the purges have on the Soviet Union?***
Was Stalin justified in carrying out the purges?

The purges

In the 1930s the Soviet Union became a totalitarian state, where a single party has power, and everyone is expected to be completely obedient to the state. All power was in the hands of the government and Stalin destroyed all opposition to his own rule. Anyone who Stalin regarded as a threat was either imprisoned or killed by the newly reorganised secret police, the NKVD, under its leader Yagoda.

This was nothing new in Russia. The tsarist secret police, the Okhrana, had imprisoned the tsar's enemies in Siberia, and Lenin had used the Cheka to destroy opposition to the Bolsheviks. However, Stalin's purges were very different. Not only were Stalin's enemies destroyed, but many of their friends and families as well. Stalin introduced a reign of terror.

The purges began after the assassination of Kirov, the party secretary in Leningrad. Within 24 hours of Kirov's assassination, the death penalty was introduced for all terrorist acts, with no possibility of pardon. The NKVD was now able to arrest and execute at will. At first, the main targets were party members. Of the 1996 delegates who attended the 1934 Party Congress, 1108 were executed in the next three years.

Source A Kirov giving a speech at the 1934 Party Conference, with Stalin looking on approvingly. A picture by Dmitri Nalbandyan, painted in 1935.

Who killed Kirov?

At 4.30 p.m. on 1 December 1934 Kirov was shot dead at the Party Headquarters in Leningrad. Who killed him? In one sense everyone agrees on their answer to this question. Kirov was killed by Nikolaev, a former member of the Communist Party, whose ex-wife worked for Kirov as a secretary. But was Nikolaev a lone assassin? Many people have suggested that Stalin had ordered Kirov's death.

Evidence that Stalin was responsible for Kirov's death

1 Nikolaev had been arrested and released twice before when found near the Party Headquarters with a gun.

2 Kirov's bodyguard, Borisov, was sent away by the NKVD on 1 December and was killed the following day. The three NKVD officers who were with him were sent to labour camps where they later died.

3 Nikolaev claimed that he was acting on NKVD orders, even after being tortured.

4 When delegates at the 1934 Party Congress voted for the members of the Central Committee of the Communist Party, Kirov had received 267 more votes than Stalin.

5 In 1989, a Soviet magazine published an extract from the memoirs of Nikita Khrushchev, who in 1934 had been the Moscow Party Secretary and a loyal supporter of Stalin. It said 'This murder was organised from above. I consider it was organised by Yagoda, who could act only on the secret instructions of Stalin, given eye to eye'. Khrushchev wrote these memoirs long after Stalin's death.

Evidence that Stalin was not responsible for Kirov's death

1 There is no evidence of any quarrel between Stalin and Kirov.

2 After Kirov's death, Stalin ordered a number of towns, as well as the Leningrad ballet company, to be named in honour of Kirov.

3 Stalin allowed Source **A** to be painted and published in *Pravda*, the Communist Party newspaper.

The show trials

In 1936 the purges spread to the leaders of the Communist Party in a series of show trials. these began with the trial of Kamenev and Zinoviev in 1936 and ended with the trial of Bukharin, the creator of the New Economic Policy, in 1938. No one was safe, not even those that carried out the purges. Yagoda was put on trial with Bukharin and was executed with him.

As Source **C** reveals, the evidence presented against the accused men was often ridiculous, and yet these senior Bolsheviks simply admitted to treason and were executed. Why did they do this? Anna Larina, Bukharin's wife, explained her husband's decision to plead guilty: 'He was a child of the party, he was devoted to it.' In other words, the party was more important than any individual, and if the party demanded that he sacrifice himself then Bukharin felt that he had no choice. He must make that sacrifice.

Trotsky did not suffer a show trial because Stalin had expelled him from Russia before the purges began. Stalin regretted this. He feared that Trotsky might still become a focus for opposition to his leadership. On 21 August 1940 Trotsky was assassinated by an NKVD agent in Mexico City.

Source C Confession of Sharangovich, Party Secretary in Byelorussia, at his trial in 1938

In 1932 we took measures to spread the plague among pigs, which resulted in the deaths of many pigs…Further, as regards…horse breeding, in 1936 we caused a wide outbreak of anaemia in Byelorussia. This was done intentionally because in Byelorussia horses are extremely important for defence purposes.

1 How does point 4 under 'Evidence that Stalin was responsible for Kirov's death' help to explain a motive for Stalin's involvement in the murder of Kirov?

2 How reliable is Khrushchev's evidence in point 5?

3 Explain why you think that Stalin was guilty or innocent.

4 In 1934 no one, not even Stalin's great enemy Trotsky, suggested that Stalin was involved in the murder of Kirov. Is it easier for historians to make judgements on what happened than it is for people at the time of the event? Use the example of Kirov's murder to support your argument.

5 What point is the cartoonist in Source **B** trying to make?

6 In what way could you consider Source **B** to be biased?

7 Why do you think people like Sharangovich and Bukharin admitted to crimes which they had not committed?

8 Source **B** is a cartoon whereas Source **C** represents the words of the accused. Does this mean Source **C** gives more reliable evidence than Source **B** about the nature of the show trials?

Questions

The armed forces

The purges were not limited to the party. In 1937 Stalin turned on the armed forces. Marshal Tukhachevsky and seven other generals, who had all been heroes of the Red Army, were quickly and secretly tried and executed. Widespread slaughter followed – 75 of the 80 men on the Supreme Military Council were executed.

The purges continued through all levels of the army – 35 000 officers were either shot or imprisoned, half the total officer force. The Soviet navy and air force were similarly treated, with every one of the admirals shot and only one air force commander left alive. This carnage crippled the armed forces at the same time that Stalin's policy of industrialisation sacrificed so many lives to ensure that Russia would be strong enough to resist invasion by the capitalist powers (see page 65).

The knock on the door

Source D Tatyana Matusevich's account of the arrest of her husband

They came at night and there was a knock on the door. 'Open the door', they shouted...I got up and the children followed me in panic. Husbands had been taken away before...we knew very well what to expect.

Source E A photograph portraying Stalin as an ordinary family man. A statue was based on the photograph and was called 'Thank you, Comrade Stalin, for my happy childhood.' In fact this girl's father was shot by the NKVD two years later.

The experience of Tatyana Matusevich, the knock on the door in the middle of the night, was one which many Russians were to have. While the show trials grabbed the headlines, the purges spread to all areas of life. Millions of ordinary Russians were arrested as people were encouraged to inform on their friends. Fourteen year-old Pavlik Morozov was made into a hero of the Revolution and statues of him were placed in many towns. He had been stabbed to death by his own family after denouncing his father to the authorities for being friendly to kulaks.

It is impossible to know exactly how many people were killed or imprisoned during this period. However, in 1988 the KGB – the Russian secret police who succeeded the NKVD – allowed some NKVD files to be examined. They suggest that between 1934 and 1939 as many as 12 million people may have died either from execution or in the labour camps. A further 12 million may also have still been alive in labour camps by 1939.

Source F A mass grave of NKVD victims at Chelyabinsk. This grave was excavated in 1989. It is believed to contain as many as 80 000 bodies.

The NKVD was arresting so many people that its prisons overflowed. Wilhelmina Slavutskaya found the prison so crowded that:

> 'We just lay the way sardines do in a can...every row had a woman who was in charge and she would give the order "Let's turn over on the other side", and the only way you could turn from one side to the other was if everyone did it together'.

Was Stalin justified?

Sources **G** and **H** give different opinions about Stalin. Read them both carefully.

Source G By a Canadian Marxist, Kenneth Cameron, in 1987

Stalin, more than any other single individual, built the first socialist society and he built it on the wreck left by the civil war...That such a man would be subjected to a concerted campaign of abuse could have been safely predicted. We could hardly have predicted its scope...Sometimes it employs simple fantasy, constructing the vision of a power mad dictator heartlessly slaughtering 'millions' (from 4 to 60 depending on the estimate).

Source H A letter to Stalin from Raskol'nikov, a Bolshevik who had fought in the October Revolution. The letter was written in 1939. Soon afterwards Raskol'nikov committed suicide.

Stalin, you have begun a new stage which will go down in the history of our revolution as the epoch of terror. No one feels safe in the Soviet Union. No one, as he goes to bed, knows whether he will escape arrest in the night...You have forced those who go along with you to walk with disgust through the pools of their comrades' and friends' blood.

Questions

1 In no more than twelve words for each, explain what Source **G** and Source **H** say about Stalin.

2 Look at Sources **D** and **F**. Do they support Source **G** or Source **H**?

3 The writers of Sources **G** and **H** are both Marxists, and yet they give very different opinions of Stalin. What reasons can you think of to explain this?

What happened to Trotsky and Yagoda?

Source A Lenin giving a speech to troops in Moscow, 5 May 1920

Source B A photograph of the same scene as in Source **A**, after Trotsky had been removed

Source **A** shows Trotsky alongside Lenin during the civil war. This is where you would expect to see Trotsky, the creator and leader of the Red Army. However, Stalin wanted to rewrite history so that there were only two Bolshevik heroes – Lenin and himself. Therefore, when this photograph was published in the Soviet Union after Trotsky's fall from power, Trotsky was missing. Removing one person, Trotsky, was straightforward. As the purges increased, there were suddenly a large number of party leaders who needed to be removed from history, often at short notice. Source **C** is an example of how this was done.

Source C *The Opening of the Belomor Canal* by Dmitri Nalbandyan, painted in 1937, with Vorishilov, Stalin and Kirov (left to right). Yagoda, who was on the right, has been removed from the painting.

Source D *A photograph of Stalin, Yagoda and Kirov on the newly-opened Belomor Canal*

As mentioned on page 65, the Belomor Canal was the first major construction project to be completed in the drive for industrialisation. As many as 100 000 people may have died while the canal was being built, but this was not something that Stalin wished to publicise. He wanted to show the Russian people how his policies were changing the Soviet Union into a modern, successful country.

Therefore, he commissioned the artist Nalbandyan to paint a huge picture to celebrate the opening of the canal (Source **C**). The painting was to feature Stalin, Yagoda and Kirov taking a trip down the newly opened canal. Having completed the picture, Nalbandyan heard that Yagoda had been arrested and was now an enemy of the people. He needed no order from Stalin to tell him to remove Yagoda. Nalbandyan knew he would be

killed if he didn't. Therefore Nalbandyan rang Vorishilov, who told the artist to take the picture to the picture restorers at the Tretyakov Gallery in Moscow. They managed to remove Yagoda and replace him with a lifebelt!

It wasn't just pictures which were altered to pretend that certain people had not existed. Nadezhda Mandelstam found that her daughter's schoolbooks were altered as well, though in a very unsubtle way, as Source **E** shows.

Source E From Nadezhda Mandelstam's memoirs

Varia...showed us her school textbooks where the portraits of the party leaders had thick pieces of paper pasted over them as one by one they fell into disgrace. This the children had to do on instructions of their teacher.

Source F *The Belomor Canal* by Pyotr Belov. Belomor became the name of a brand of cigarettes. The artist painted this picture long after Stalin's death.

Questions

1 Nalbandyan had to remove Yagoda from the painting in Source **C**. Why was it not necessary for him to remove Kirov as well?

2 In Source **A** the figure behind Trotsky is Kamenev. Why would it be necessary to remove him from the photograph as well?

3 What was Stalin's purpose in changing photographs and paintings?

4 Was the Belomor Canal worth it?
a) What impression of the Belomor Canal do you get from Source **C**?
b) What point do you think that the artist is making in Source **F**?
c) Look at Source **H** on page 65. Does it support Source **C** or Source **F**?
d) What reasons can you think of to explain the different opinions of the building of the Belomor Canal shown in Sources **C** and **F**?

Life in Stalin's Russia

▶ ## What was it like to live and work in Russia in the 1930s?

The cult of Stalin

There were statues of Stalin in every town, pictures of him in every shop and factory. The small peasant hut in which he grew up was preserved in a temple-like structure. Every success was claimed to be due to his great genius. Any failures were blamed on others. This became known as the cult of Stalin. He was treated like a god who was leading his people to the promised land of socialism. Socialism was presented as the future, and capitalism as old and outdated.

Look back to page 13 and you will see that, according to Marx, socialism is the stage following after capitalism. What better way to show this than to use modern technology? In the 1930s, Stalin ordered an underground rail system – the metro – to be built in Moscow. In a city with so few cars there was no need for a metro. It was not being built to meet traffic needs, but to show the success of socialism. The stations were elaborate and luxurious. Nothing like it had ever been built in the capitalist West. At the same time, huge new buildings began to appear in Russia. In the West this new style of architecture was mockingly called 'wedding cake' architecture. However, it was huge and looked impressive. Stalin planned to build the highest building in the world, capped with a 100 metre-high statue of Lenin, but it was never built.

Source A The celebrations for Stalin's 70th birthday. A huge picture of Stalin hangs over Red Square as if by magic. In fact it is hanging from a balloon.

Source B ▶
Moscow State University. An example of the massive 'wedding cake' architecture built by Stalin.

Source C A speech given by the writer, A. Avdienko in 1935
▼

Thank you, Stalin. Thank you because I am joyful. Thank you because I am well…Centuries will pass, and the generations still to come will regard us as the happiest of mortals, as the most fortunate of men…because we were privileged to see Stalin…We regard ourselves as the happiest of mortals because we live at the same time as a man who never had an equal in world history.

Housing

While vast amounts of money were being spent on projects like the metro, very little was being spent on new houses for the workers. Industrialisation was drawing more and more peasants into the cities, but there was nowhere for them to live. In Moscow only 6 per cent of families had lived in more than one room, and 25 per cent of families lived more than one family to a room. As in the days before the revolution, most unmarried workers still lived in dormitories.

Education

In 1917 the vast majority of the Russian people were illiterate – that is, they could not read or write. The Bolsheviks regarded this lack of education as one of the ways in which the ruling class had controlled the workers and peasants. In a socialist state, education would be available to all. Lunacharsky was made Commissar for Education and he worked closely with Lenin's widow, Krupskaya.

The Party Congress of 1919 laid down plans for compulsory education for all up to the age of 17. This was an enormous task, but by 1927 education was being provided for everyone up to the age of 12. Modern western theories of education were introduced. Examinations were abolished, as were reports. Pupils were encouraged to learn by carrying out projects rather than by formal learning from the teacher. The standard type of school was the polytechnic, which was a comprehensive school which all children attended. Before the Revolution few girls had received an education.

Work was done to educate adults who had missed out during their childhood. Source **D** is a government poster encouraging adults to join classes teaching workers and peasants to read and write. A census of 1939 revealed that 94 per cent of 9–49 year-olds living in towns were literate, as were 86 per cent of those living in villages. Rabfaks were also created. These were classes which tried to bring workers up to the standard where they could go on to higher education. Many of the next generation of leaders, such as Nikita Khrushchev, were educated in Rabfaks.

In the 1930s, education was purged along with everything else. Lunacharsky was dismissed and with him went his 'progressive' ideas on education.

Source D 'You might as well be blind as illiterate' – a government poster, 1920

Examinations were brought back and teachers were encouraged to discipline pupils. Standard textbooks were introduced so that everyone learnt the same things from the same books, and Stalin could control exactly what they learnt. (Look at Source **E** on page 71 to see what happened to school textbooks.) There was now less money available for education, and while primary schooling remained free, fees were introduced for the last three years of secondary school, making it much more difficult for the children of poor people to get a good education.

Censorship

Stalin kept a strict eye on all writers and artists to make sure that they followed strict party guidelines. Whereas Lenin had merely preferred painters to adopt a realistic approach which glorified socialism, under Stalin this 'socialist realism' was the only style allowed in both writing and art. Failure to do so meant imprisonment. The writer Alexander Solzhenitsyn spent eight years in a labour camp. His novel based on his experiences there, *A Day in the Life of Ivan Denisovitch*, was banned and not published in the Soviet Union until long after Stalin's death.

Source E *A feast on a collective farm* by Gerasimov, 1937. An example of socialist realism.

The constitution of 1936

In 1936 the communists produced their third constitution. The first had been produced in a hurry in 1918, and this had been replaced in 1924 by the constitution which created the USSR, a union of national republics. The 1936 constitution was written by Bukharin and was described by Stalin as the 'most democratic in the world'. The constitution guaranteed the people certain rights, including freedom of speech and freedom of religion. However this did not really help the people, since the Politburo and the NKVD were not controlled by the constitution and so could do whatever they wanted.

Questions

1 Source **E** shows an example of a socialist realist painting. In what ways does it glorify socialism?

2 How reliable is Source **E** as evidence of the state of Russian agriculture? (Look back to page 52.)

3 How do you think the people of the USSR would have reacted to the extravagant celebration of Stalin's 70th birthday?

Consider the following groups of people and think how they would all feel. For example:
a) Loyal party members (look at Source **C**),
b) Workers living one family to a room,
c) Peasants – they had suffered from collectivisation and then severe famine in 1931–2,
d) The army,
e) Prisoners in the labour camps,
f) Families of people who had been arrested or killed,
g) Christians and Jews (see page 49).

The Great Patriotic War

Why were the Russians able to defeat Germany?
What was the effect of the Second World War on Russia?

The war which we in the West call the Second World War is known in Russia as the Great Patriotic War. The difference is important. Hitler believed that the Russians were a subhuman people who deserved to become the slaves of the superior Germans. Twenty million Russians died to prevent this happening, in a war that was unbelievably savage.

The Nazi-Soviet Pact, August 1939

The western world was shocked when, on 23 August 1939, Fascist Germany and communist Russia signed a non-aggression pact in which they promised not to attack one another. Secretly, the Russians and Germans also agreed to divide Poland between them. The Russians were to be allowed to recover all the land they had lost in the Treaty of Brest-Litovsk, in return for supplying Germany with oil and other vital commodities. It was not just the West which was caught unprepared. When the German Foreign Minister, von Ribbentrop, arrived in Moscow to sign the treaty, the only German flags which could be found were in a film studio where they were being used to produce an anti-fascist film.

Stalin felt he had no choice. The policy of rapid industrialisation had been launched because Stalin was sure the capitalist powers would one day invade Russia. The Fascist take-over of Germany clearly showed that the invasion would be a German one. Between 1936 and 1939 Britain and France continually gave in to Hitler rather than declare war on him. Stalin believed this meant they would not attack Hitler if he invaded Russia. Therefore, in signing the pact with Germany, Stalin was turning the tables on Britain and France. He promised that Russia would remain neutral if Hitler attacked Britain and France. Stalin regarded the pact as a masterstroke. Russia was not strong enough to defeat Germany in 1939, but Stalin was certain that Germany would not attack Russia until Britain and France had been defeated. Then Russia would be able to take on a Germany already weakened by war.

All seemed to go according to plan. On 1 September 1939 Germany invaded Poland and destroyed the Polish army. Britain and France declared

Source A Cartoon by David Low from the *Evening Standard*, November 1939. The caption reads 'Someone is taking someone for a walk'.

war on Germany on 3 September. Fourteen days later the Red Army was able to occupy Eastern Poland virtually unopposed. By 1941 The Red Army had recaptured all the areas lost in the Treaty of Brest-Litovsk. The Red Army were followed by the NKVD, who arrested thousands of 'opponents' before despatching them to Russian labour camps.

Questions

1 Look at Source **A**. What point is the cartoonist making about the Nazi-Soviet pact?

2 What evidence is there in the text to support the cartoonist's view?

3 A cartoon only represents the view of the cartoonist. Does that mean it is of no use to a historian? Give reasons for your answer.

Operation Barbarossa

At 4.15 a.m. on 22 June 1941 about 3.2 million German troops poured into Russia. Stalin had miscalculated. Even though Britain had not been defeated, Hitler had launched his invasion of Russia, code-named Operation Barbarossa. The Red Army was caught unprepared and greatly weakened through the recent purges of its officers. Fifteen years later, Khrushchev revealed that Stalin had ignored warnings that Hitler was about to launch an attack. He had been certain it would not occur until Britain and France were defeated.

By noon the German air force, the *Luftwaffe*, had destroyed 1200 Russian aircraft, almost all of them still on the ground. The Germans quickly regained the lands which the Russians had taken back after the 1939 pact. Where there was transport available, the NKVD packed its prisoners off to the labour camps. Where there was no transport the prisoners were killed. When the Germans arrived in Lvov on 29 June they found the prisons full of the remains of thousands of Russian prisoners, all of whom had been slaughtered during the previous seven days. The German army was accompanied by the SS, Hitler's private army, who treated the people with incredible cruelty. In a single massacre at Babi Yar, near Kiev, 100 000 Jews were slaughtered.

By October the Germans were in sight of Moscow and victory, but they got no further. Two major factors were responsible for this:

1   As the Russians retreated, Stalin ordered them to adopt a 'scorched earth' policy. As many as 1360 factories were taken to pieces and reconstructed east of the Urals. Farm animals were marched to the east. Anything which could not be taken was destroyed. The further the Germans advanced into Russia, the longer it took for supplies to reach them from Germany. It also meant that the Russians could still produce the weapons and ammunition that were needed to continue the war.

2   The Russian weather. In October it poured with rain, turning the ground into mud which slowed the German advance. In November, the temperatures dropped to -28 degrees in a winter which was bad even by Russian standards. The German soldiers were not dressed or equipped for such conditions, and many froze to death. German vehicles also froze and would not work.

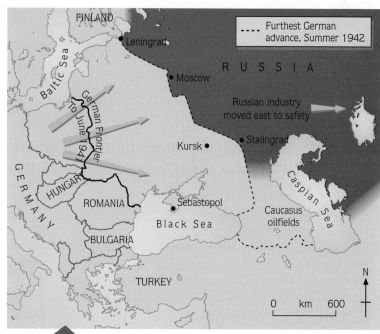

Source B   Map of Operation Barbarossa

Stalingrad

Stalingrad was the crucial battle of the Great Patriotic War. In 1942 Hitler launched an attack intended to capture the vital Russian oil wells. Against the advice of his generals, Hitler ordered that the city of Stalingrad be captured first. He knew that it would be a serious blow to Russian morale to lose a city which was named after their leader.

General von Paulus attacked with a force of 400 000 men. The outnumbered Russian forces fought a guerrilla war with soldiers fighting in small groups defending each building in turn. The Russian Army newspaper *Red Star* reported 'Often it happens that while the enemy holds one part of a building, we hold another'. As was often the case in the first 18 months of the war, the Russian army relied on the willingness of its troops to die. As a German general later commented 'The Russian soldier values his own life no more than his comrade's. Life is not precious to him'.

Source C   Stalingrad at the end of the battle. Virtually nothing remained.

Stalingrad was reduced to rubble, but the Russians held on until the winter, when a huge Russian army led by Marshal Zhukov advanced on Stalingrad and surrounded it. The German army was bottled up with no hope of escape, and on 2 February 1943 they surrendered. In all 200 000 German troops had died, and we have no idea of the Russian casualties.

The Battle of Stalingrad was vital to Russian morale because it proved that they could defeat the Germans. Six months later Hitler tried to fight back by involving all of his heavy tanks in a battle at Kursk. Under Zhukov's command, 1.3 million Russian soldiers and 3000 tanks forced the Germans to retreat. The Germans were outnumbered and their tanks were outclassed by the more mobile Russian T3 tanks. These would never have been built if Russian industry had not been moved east of the Ural Mountains.

Now the Red Army was winning the fight, and the long, slow push to Berlin had begun. More and more territory was recaptured from the retreating Germans, who carried out the same 'scorched earth' policy that the Russians had used on their retreat into Russia.

Source D 'Long live the Red Army – loyal guard of the October Revolution'. A Russian government poster from 1933.

Source E 'We're Suvorov's descendants, Chapayev's children'. A Russian government poster from 1941 which uses the memory of Russian heroes from long before the Revolution.

If Stalingrad was the turning point of the war, Leningrad represented the greatest heroism of the war. For almost 900 days from 1941 to 1944 Leningrad was surrounded. Three million people were trapped inside the city, with very little food. People ate anything they could find, even scraping the glue from the back of wallpaper. Dogs and cats fetched high prices. About 700 000 citizens died of cold and starvation and a further 200 000 were killed in German bombing, but the city managed to hold out.

Source F 'Bombs made beyond the Urals destroy the German army'. A soviet poster from 1942.

Questions

Source **E** does not ask the Russian people to fight the Germans to defend communism, but to defend Russia. This is very different to Source **D**, which sees the Red Army as the defenders of communism.
a) What does this tell you about what the Russian people thought of the Communist Party by 1941?
b) What might have brought about this change of attitude?

Economic production

For much of the war most of Russia west of the Ural Mountains was occupied by the Germans. Millions of men were called up by the Red Army. Women and unskilled workers had to be used to fill their jobs. By 1942, Russian economic production had declined to 77 per cent of the 1940 level, but by 1944 it had actually managed to achieve 104 per cent of 1940 industrial output.

In other words, Russian industry was actually managing to produce more during the war than it had in peacetime. This shows the success of Stalin's policy of moving industry to the east of the Urals. Russia produced twice as many rifles and machine guns as Germany during the war, and more of every major category of weapon.

Source G The Russian attack on the Germans at Sebastopol, painted in 1944–7

Agriculture was a different story. Grain harvests in 1942 and 1943 were half those of 1940. So many horses were sent to the army that women often had to pull the plough. The Russian people went very hungry throughout the war.

Source H *Stalin as War Leader* by Pyotr Belov, painted in the 1980s

1 **a)** Source **G** shows the Russian attack on the German positions above Sebastopol. What impression of the Russian war effort are the artists attempting to show?

2 What impression is the artist of Source **H** trying to give about Stalin's tactics?
What evidence can you find in the text to support this?

3 Why do you think the two paintings give such a different view?

4 After the war, many people regarded Stalin as the saviour of Russia and the man mainly responsible for the defeat of Hitler. Is this fair?
Read through this chapter and write down the evidence:
a) which suggests that Stalin's policies helped to win the war for Russia.
b) which suggest that his policies made a Russian victory more difficult to achieve.
In particular you should note:
- The purges of the armed forces
- The Nazi-Soviet Pact,
- Industrial policy,
- Khrushchev's evidence

Questions

Russia as a superpower

The beginning of the Cold War

Why did the Cold War break out?
Was the Cold War caused by Russian aggression?

The Grand Alliance

The Second World War with Germany had forced Germany's enemies – Russia, Britain and America – to join together. This was known as the Grand Alliance. Britain and America supplied Russia with weapons while Stalin dissolved Comintern (see page 36).

However, Stalin did not trust his Western allies. He had signed the Nazi-Soviet Pact in 1939 because he believed Britain and France would not help prevent a German attack on Russia. Events during the war seemed to confirm Stalin's suspicions. While the Red Army coped with the full might of the German army, Stalin pleaded with Britain and America to open a second front in Western Europe. This would force the Germans to withdraw troops from Russia. The British and the Americans promised to open a second front, but only when they were sure it would succeed. To Stalin it seemed that they were content for Russians to die in large numbers so long as it saved British and American lives.

When the British and Americans did finally open a second front with the invasion of France, it was in June 1944. By then it was far too late for the Russians. They had already driven the Germans out of Russia, but only after enormous loss of life.

The leaders of the Grand Alliance met twice in 1945 – first in the Russian town of Yalta and then, once the Germans had surrendered, in the Berlin suburb of Potsdam. They agreed to allow Russia to regain all the land that had been lost at Brest-Litovsk (see page 35). To make sure that Germany would not be strong enough to start another war, they agreed to divide it into four sectors, each controlled by one of the four Allied powers, including France – now freed from German control by the Allied forces.

The origins of the Cold War

During the Second World War, the major nations of the world had fought one another all over the globe. At the start of the twentieth century there were a number of powerful countries, including Russia, who were known as the Great Powers. After the Second World War there were two countries – the USA and the USSR – who were far more powerful than the rest.

Source A
Soldiers killed during the Second World War

265,000
292,000
7-10 million

They were known as the superpowers.

Each of the superpowers believed that the other was trying to dominate the world. They were therefore very hostile to one another, but neither could face the death and destruction which would occur if they declared war on one another. The Cold War had begun.

However, the two superpowers were not equal. American industry had supplied huge quantities of weapons to Britain and Russia. As a result, the US economy was booming. In contrast, the Russian economy had been initially destroyed by the German invasion. Stalin was well aware that the Russians were in no position to threaten America. The United States had the atom bomb, and could destroy the Soviet Union if they wished. At the end of the Second World War, Stalin had three clear aims:

1 To develop an atom bomb so that the United States could no longer threaten Russia. This was the theory of 'nuclear deterrent'. If both sides had the atom bomb then neither could use it, as this would lead to both sides being destroyed.
2 To repair the Soviet Union's economy. As the economy had been destroyed by Germany, it seemed only fair that the cost should be borne by Germany and her allies.
3 To ensure that Russia could never again be invaded from Europe. Stalin wanted there to be communist governments in the countries of Eastern Europe so that the Red Army could be stationed there. This would be a buffer zone between Russia and Western Europe.

How successful was Stalin in achieving these aims?

1 In 1949 Russia detonated an atom bomb.

2 Stalin dismantled the machinery and factories of the Russian sector of Germany to be taken back to Russia.

3 Between 1945 and 1948 Russia took control of Eastern Europe.

Source B Map of Eastern Europe after the Second World War. By 1948 Stalin had achieved his aim. There were communist governments in every country of Eastern Europe.

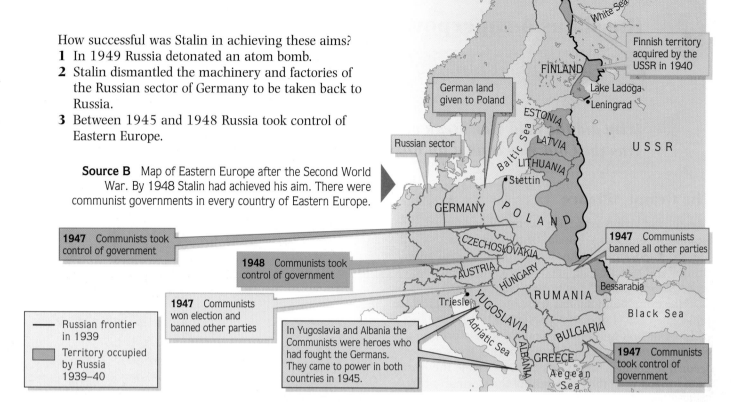

Finnish territory acquired by the USSR in 1940

German land given to Poland

Russian sector

1947 Communists took control of government

1948 Communists took control of government

1947 Communists won election and banned other parties

1947 Communists banned all other parties

1947 Communists took control of government

In Yugoslavia and Albania the Communists were heroes who had fought the Germans. They came to power in both countries in 1945.

— Russian frontier in 1939

Territory occupied by Russia 1939–40

The Truman Doctrine and Marshall Aid

Britain and America felt they had fought the Second World War in order to prevent a dictator – Adolf Hitler – from taking over Europe. The Russian domination of Eastern Europe now seemed to be leading to exactly that. Harry Truman, the new US President, shared Churchill's fears (Source **C**). In order to prevent a Russian takeover of Europe he announced that '...it must be the policy of the United States to support free peoples who are resisting armed takeover...by outside pressure'. This was known as the Truman Doctrine.

Source C Winston Churchill speaking at Fulton, Missouri, in March 1946

A shadow has fallen upon the scene lately lighted by the Allied victory...From Stettin, in the Baltic, to Trieste, in the Adriatic, an Iron Curtain has descended across the continent. Behind that lie all the capitals of the states of central and eastern Europe. All those famous cities and the populations around them lie in the Soviet sphere and are all subject, in one way or another, to a very high and increasing measure of control from Moscow.

Source D Stalin's reply to Churchill's Fulton speech

The following circumstances should not be forgotten. The Germans made their invasion of the USSR through Finland, Poland, Rumania, Bulgaria and Hungary...The Soviet Union's loss of life has been several times greater than that of Britain and the United States put together. And so what can be surprising about the fact that the Soviet Union, anxious for its future safety, is trying to see to it that governments loyal to the Soviet Union should exist in those countries.

1 What does Churchill mean by the phrase 'an Iron Curtain'?

2 In what way does Source **D** contradict Source **C**?

3 In what way does Source **D** support Source **C**?

4 Does Churchill consider Russian control of Eastern Europe to be acceptable or not? Explain your answer.

5 What evidence can you find to support Stalin's view, expressed in Source **D**?

6 How do Sources **C** and **D** help to explain why the Cold War broke out?

7 Who was to blame for the outbreak of the Cold War? Make a list of those causes which were the fault of Russia, and a separate list of those that were the fault of Britain and America. Then use these to decide who you think was to blame.

Questions

Source E A German poster – 'The Marshall Plan is available to all countries. National borders do not limit it'.

In 1947 the US Secretary of State (Foreign Minister) George Marshall announced a plan to give billions of dollars in aid to help rebuild Europe. Any country, even Russia, would be able to apply for this aid. Why were the Americans willing to do this?

America was the world's leading trading nation. To remain prosperous, America needed to be able to trade with Europe, but the war had destroyed the economies of almost all the countries of Europe. So the Plan was in America's own interest. America also feared that if the people of Europe were allowed to remain in poverty they would turn to communism, and this would allow Russia to dominate Europe.

Stalin considered accepting Marshall Aid. The Russian economy desperately needed the billions of dollars the Americans were offering. But Stalin decided that it would make Russia dependant upon America and therefore weaker. Stalin did not allow the countries of Eastern Europe to accept Marshall Aid. But Eastern Europe needed help, and so in 1949 the Russians set up Comecon, which was Russian-backed economic aid for Eastern Europe. However, given the economic condition of Russia, the countries of Eastern Europe received much less money from Comecon than they would have from Marshall Aid.

Source F Map showing the location of Berlin and the division of Germany

Berlin

Berlin was the capital of Germany. After the war it was divided into four sectors, just like Germany itself. However, Berlin was located deep inside the Russian sector of Germany. This meant there were American, British and French troops a long way inside the Russian sector – behind what Stalin considered to be the Russian front line in the event of a future invasion of Russia.

In 1948 Stalin ordered that all road and rail links to Berlin be cut. In America this was seen as another example of Russian aggression. America kept Berlin supplied by air, so that Russia failed to drive the Western troops out of Berlin. In June 1949 Stalin backed down and reopened the land links into Berlin.

To the countries in the West, the Berlin blockade seemed to prove that the Soviet Union was attempting to take over Europe. Therefore, in 1949, America formed a military alliance with the countries of Western Europe so that together they would be strong enough to defeat Soviet aggression. This was NATO – the North Atlantic Treaty Organisation. Six years later, Russia responded by setting up the Warsaw Pact, a military alliance of Russia with all the countries of Eastern Europe.

Questions

1 Source **E** shows that Marshall Aid was available to the countries of Eastern Europe. Why was Stalin able to stop them accepting it?

2 President Truman called Marshall Aid 'one of America's greatest contributions to the peace of the world'. Explain whether you agree or disagree with this statement.

Khrushchev: a reform of Stalinism?

▶ **How much did the policies of the Soviet Union change after the death of Stalin? Did life improve for the people of Russia after Stalin died?**

A new leader

In March 1953 Stalin died. His body was preserved and put on display alongside that of Lenin. Just as in 1924 after the death of Lenin, a struggle for power took place. The three main contenders were the Prime Minister, Malenkov, the Party Secretary, Khrushchev, and the Foreign Minister, Molotov, the only one who had been an important member of the party before the Revolution.

By 1958 Khrushchev had won this battle for the leadership. Like Stalin 30 years earlier, Khrushchev's main strength was his position as Party Secretary. In the years after Stalin's death he had promoted his own supporters and so was in a stronger position than his opponents.

Khrushchev believed he had a mission to lead the people of Russia and create a truly communist state (see page 13). This state would have food, goods and justice for all. It would happen within just 20 years. To achieve this, Khrushchev did not use the terror tactics of Stalin. He wanted to reform the system so that it worked better. When more food and consumer goods were produced, the people would be convinced and so force would not be needed. He immediately released 705 inmates of the gulags. However, when Khrushchev's reforms did not work his only response was to introduce new reforms. This made him very unpopular with the party officials who had to carry out his orders. They did not like so much change.

The Twentieth Party Congress, 1956

Khrushchev stunned the world when he made a six-hour speech to the Twentieth Party Congress. Khrushchev described Stalin as a 'criminal murderer' who had ordered the deaths of many thousands of loyal communists. Khrushchev blamed this on the cult of personality which had given people the impression that Stalin was:

> '...a superman possessing supernatural character-istics like those of a god. Such a man supposedly knows everything, thinks for everyone, can do anything.'

Khrushchev also described Stalin as 'capricious and despotic', that is unpredictable and a tyrant. Finally, Khrushchev suggested a major change of policy – an end to the Cold War. In an age when both superpowers possessed nuclear weapons:

> 'There are only two ways – either peaceful co-existence or the most destructive war in history.'

Khrushchev seemed to be proposing a complete change from the tyranny of the Stalin years. But is this really what happened?

Peaceful co-existence?

Source A 'No!' A Soviet poster backing Khrushchev's policy of peaceful co-existence, 1958

The Cold War did not end. Certainly Khrushchev adopted a much more co-operative style. He travelled to the West to meet US President Eisenhower and his successor President Kennedy. This seemed very different to the aggressive approach used by Stalin. However, Stalin had been trying to establish firm control of Eastern Europe in order to protect Russia from invasion (see page 80). Events were to prove that Khrushchev was no different.

In both Poland and Hungary the leaders thought that Khrushchev's speech against Stalin meant that the tight Soviet control over their countries was now over. Gomulka became the new leader of Poland and Nagy became leader in Hungary. Both men had been banned from office by Stalin. In Hungary, statues of Stalin were torn down by protesters and Nagy proposed both free elections and that Hungary should leave the Warsaw Pact. This would totally undermine the defence of Russia. On 4 November 1956 1000 Red Army tanks moved into Hungary and the Russians were back in control. Nagy and the other leaders of the Hungarian government were shot. At least 20 000 Hungarians were killed by Soviet troops.

The Berlin Wall, 1961

A similar pattern can be seen in Khrushchev's actions over Berlin. West Berlin received Western aid and soon developed a standard of living as high as any in Europe. It was surrounded by the poverty of East Germany. Between 1949 and 1957 over two million Germans fled from the Russian sector into West Berlin. This loss of skilled manpower threatened to destroy the economy of East Germany, as the Russian sector was called. Therefore, in 1961, Khrushchev allowed the East German government to build a wall between East and West Berlin. Anyone attempting to cross the wall was shot dead. Khrushchev's policy in Eastern Europe was no different to Stalin's. There was to be no peaceful co-existence.

The Cuban Missile Crisis, 1962

With Khrushchev's reforms going badly in Russia, he looked for a victory against the USA. In 1959 the pro-American government of the Caribbean island of Cuba was overthrown by a group of revolutionaries led by Fidel Castro. Castro was not a communist, but his policy of giving the land to the peasants looked like communism to the US government. America threatened to stop buying Cuban sugar, and in 1960 Castro signed a trade treaty with the USSR. Russia promised to buy Cuba's sugar.

In 1962 American spy planes discovered that the Russians were building bases on Cuba for nuclear missiles. President Kennedy ordered Khrushchev to remove them. The world held its breath as nuclear war seemed possible. After two weeks it was Khrushchev who backed down and ordered the missiles to be removed, although both sides claimed a victory.

Source B Hungarians destroy a statue of Stalin in Budapest, 1956. It was actions such as these which worried the Soviet leaders.

Source C Looking over the Berlin Wall

Source D The range of the missiles on Cuba

Soviet missile bases

US naval blockade

Agriculture

'What sort of Communism is it that cannot provide sausage?'
Khrushchev

In 1953 Khrushchev reported to the Central Committee of the Communist Party that grain stocks were lower than they had been in tsarist times. Despite collectivisation, the Soviet Union was still not growing enough food. Khrushchev introduced two policies to improve this situation:
● The 'virgin lands' policy,
● Financial assistance to peasants.

Most adventurous was the 'virgin lands' policy. Huge areas of Kazakhstan and Siberia which had never before been used for agriculture were to be planted with food crops. Like Stalin's industrialisation, this was to be a crusade, and over a quarter of a million young communists volunteered to take part in the scheme.

At first it seemed to be a success. However, food crops such as maize were being grown on soil that was unsuitable. The result was an ecological disaster. There was not enough rain, and in 1963 Kazakhstan became a dust bowl. Hurricane force winds ripped the topsoil from six million hectares of land and deposited it on the foothills of the Sayan Mountains. Russia was forced to buy grain from America and Australia to prevent famine.

Source E Khrushchev examining crops. As the son of a peasant, Khrushchev regarded himself as an expert on agriculture, although he had not been a farmer himself.

Khrushchev's other policy was to cut taxes on farming profits and for the government to pay peasants higher prices for their food crops. This was a return to Lenin's New Economic Policy. Peasants were being encouraged to grow more food by the prospect of real rewards. However, this would only work if Soviet industry produced more consumer goods for the peasants to buy with their profits.

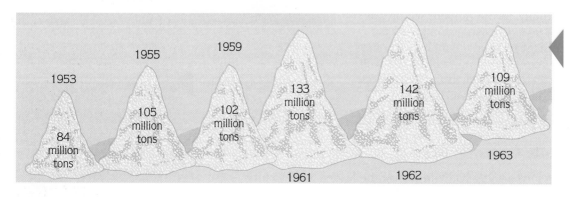

Source F Russian grain harvest under Khrushchev, 1953–63

1953 — 84 million tons
1955 — 105 million tons
1959 — 102 million tons
1961 — 133 million tons
1962 — 142 million tons
1963 — 109 million tons

Source G Report from a member of the American government who visited Russia in the 1950s

Huge piles of grain lay in the open on roads and on farms without any sort of covering. Russian workers turned this grain by hand to help it dry. Buckets, trowels and saucepans…were used in this operation…It was raining and I know that much of the crop was lost.

The purpose of Khrushchev's policies was to grow more food.
a) Look at Source **F**. Was he successful? Give your reasons.
b) Look at Source **G**. What does this suggest were the real problems of Russian agriculture?
c) What effect would the problems described in Source **G** have on Khrushchev's policies?

Questions

Industry

Khrushchev wanted a major change in industrial production, with priority given to producing consumer goods to give Russians a higher standard of living. This proved very difficult to achieve. The Arms Race between the Soviet Union and America meant that defence spending took up more and more money, and on top of this came the demands of the Space Race. Khrushchev realised that the conquest of space offered the chance for Russia to prove to the world that she had overtaken America. Therefore, vast amounts of money were spent and spectacular successes were achieved.

In 1957 Russia stunned America by putting Sputnik, the first ever man-made satellite, into orbit around the earth. Four years later America was again beaten when Yuri Gagarin became the first man in space.

However, this was achieved at some cost. While Gagarin was in space, Russian shop assistants still used the abacus, a counting frame invented thousands of years ago.

Source H The front page of the *Daily Mirror*, an English newspaper, 13 April 1961

Source I Comparative figures for consumer goods ownership in Russia and the USA. Figures are the number of items for every 1000 people.

		USSR 1955	USSR 1966	USA 1966
Motor cars		2	5	398
TV sets		4	82	376
Refrigerators		4	40	293
Washing machines		1	77	259

Source J An American's view of Khrushchev, written in 1962 by John Gunther

Since early 1955 Khrushchev has changed Russia irreversibly…it is impossible not to agree that there have been tremendous changes for the better since Stalin's day.

Questions

1 Why did Khrushchev spend so much money on the exploration of space?

2 Look at Source **H**. Why do you think that Khrushchev would have been pleased with the coverage of Gagarin's flight?

3 Do you think that the people of Russia would have been sad to see Khrushchev dismissed as leader? Decide how each of the following would have felt:
   a) peasants,
   b) people living in the cities,
   c) military leaders,
   d) government officials.

4 a) What evidence can you find to support Source **J**?
   b) What evidence can you find in this unit which does not support Source **J**?
   c) Do you think that Source **J** is an accurate verdict on Khrushchev? Use the information you have gathered for parts **a)** and **b)** to explain your answer.

The Brezhnev Years: an age of stagnation?

 Was Brezhnev a successful leader?

A new era

In 1964 Khrushchev was replaced. The men he had promoted now stepped into his shoes. What had gone wrong? The party newspaper *Pravda* accused him of 'hare-brained scheme-making, of half-baked conclusions and hasty decisions and actions.' The virgin lands policy and the Cuban Missiles Crisis, it said, were just two examples of these. Khrushchev's constant changing of policy was too much for the nomenklatura (see information box). After the terror of Stalin and the risk-taking of Khrushchev, they wanted stability so that they could enjoy their superior lifestyle. Once more a group of leaders took over. Andrei Kosygin took over as Prime Minister, but by 1968 Leonid Brezhnev had emerged as the dominant figure.

Later, in the 1980s, President Gorbachev criticised the rule of Brezhnev as an age of stagnation, when the problems of the Soviet Union were allowed to grow and nothing was done about them. However, since Khrushchev, it has become normal for Soviet leaders to criticise the leaders who had come before them. Were the Brezhnev years really so bad?

Nomenklatura

These people were the Russian ruling class. From the very start, Lenin believed that being a loyal communist was more important than technical skills when choosing important officials. These people took all the key decisions, and, along with their families, they formed around one per cent of the population. Their reward was a much higher standard of living than other Russians.

Source A Brezhnev with US President Jimmy Carter at the SALT II conference in 1979. Brezhnev had already suffered two strokes by this stage and was very weak.

Victory for the nomenklatura

Khrushchev had regularly replaced officials with people of his own choosing. He hoped this would ensure that his reforms were successful. But it simply upset the nomenklatura. Under Brezhnev, officials stayed in their jobs for a long time, and when they did stand down they were generally replaced by their deputies. As a result the average age of officials increased. This was very obvious in the Politburo. When Brezhnev died in 1982, all but two of its members were old age pensioners. Under Brezhnev, the nomenklatura were able to settle down to a stable and comfortable existence. It was very rare for any official to be demoted.

However, this easy life led to increasing corruption and bribery, which went to the very centre of the government. Even Brezhnev's own daughter, Galina, and her husband General Yuri Cherbanov were involved.

Détente

Brezhnev continued Khrushchev's policy of peaceful co-existence, or at least a *competitive* co-existence. The Space Race continued, although the Russians lost when the Americans landed Neil Armstrong and Buzz Aldrin on the moon in 1969. The Arms Race continued as well. Under Brezhnev, the Soviet Union built the most powerful navy in the world. In 1966 the Americans developed a missile with a multiple nuclear warhead, and the Russians did the same two years later. In 1970 the Americans developed the technology to target these warheads independently, so that one missile could attack a number of cities. In 1978 the Russians developed this capability as well.

In a policy known as détente, Brezhnev began a series of talks with the Americans. Détente was a lessening of the tension between the USA and the Soviet Union. If the two superpowers were in regular contact it lessened the chance of nuclear war. It also meant that the Soviet Union was able to import grain from the USA to make up for its own shortage, and import the high technology needed to modernise Soviet industry. An example of détente came in 1972 when Brezhnev met US President Nixon and signed the SALT (Strategic Arms Limitation Talks) agreement which limited the spread of nuclear weapons. In reality, SALT had little effect on the Arms Race, since it did not stop the development of new weapons.

Source C   A Czech poster from 1968

The Prague Spring, 1968

Policy towards Eastern Europe showed that the security of the Soviet Union was still vital. In January 1968 the Communist Party in Czechoslovakia elected a new leader, Alexander Dubček. He immediately introduced a whole series of reforms, including ending censorship of the press and allowing the free discussion of political ideas. However, Dubček also stressed that he had no intention of leaving the Warsaw Pact. The Czechs felt that it was this threat that had forced the Russians to invade Hungary in 1956. By staying in the Warsaw Pact they would not be weakening the defence of Russia, and so they believed that the Russians would allow them to introduce their reforms, known as 'Socialism with a human face.' It was not to be.

Brezhnev finally decided to support an invasion of Czechoslovakia when the reforms threatened the continuation of communism. Half a million Warsaw Pact troops invaded in August 1968. The Czechs did not attempt to fight. They were completely outnumbered.

Source B   Czechs wander around Russian tanks in Prague

Questions

1 What does Source **B** tell you about the Russian invasion of Czechoslovakia?

2 What does Source **C** tell you of how the Czechs felt about the invasion?

3 Do you think that the poster or the photograph is more useful in helping you to understand how the Czechs felt about being invaded by Russia? Explain your answer.

Agriculture

One of the main criticisms of Khrushchev was that he had failed to solve the problems of Soviet agriculture. Under Brezhnev, up to 30 per cent of government investment was spent in trying to improve agricultural performance. The results were still a failure. In 1975 the grain harvest was only 140 million tonnes, which was only 67 per cent of the target. The Russians were forced to buy grain regularly from the Americans after 1975, just like Khrushchev had had to do in 1963.

The standard of living

To try and keep the people contented, Brezhnev needed to improve the standard of living of ordinary people. The Five Year Plans tried to ensure that, for the first time, the production of consumer goods was greater than production of heavy industrial goods. However, the targets were not met. Despite this, Sources **D** and **E** clearly show that people were able to buy far more consumer goods than ever before.

Wages rose by about 50 per cent during the Brezhnev years. Also, a five-day working week was introduced in 1967, and the following year the national minimum wage was increased to 60 rubles a month. Before, the minimum wage had been set at 50 rubles a month, less than the level necessary to buy the basic necessities of life. In particular the workers on the collective farms benefited. In 1965, 75 per cent of all collective farm workers earned less than 50 rubles a month. For the first time, older collective farm workers were allowed to retire and receive a pension. However, it was only 12 rubles a month. Even after they had retired, farm workers were expected to grow their own food. Paying the collective farm workers more would have put up the cost of food, and this would have made the government very unpopular with the people in the towns. To stop this happening, the government had to spend more and more money subsidising the price of food, to make up the difference between the price of food in the shops and the price paid to farmers. By 1979 this came to 20 billion rubles a year – more than the Russian defence budget!

Even this did not keep the people happy. The farms were still not meeting their targets. Although people had more money to spend, there was no more food in the shops to spend it on.

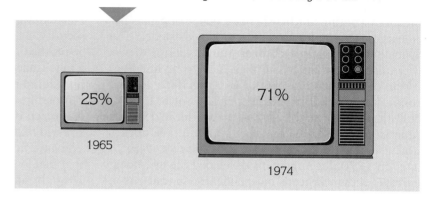

Source D Percentage of Russians owning a TV set

25% 1965

71% 1974

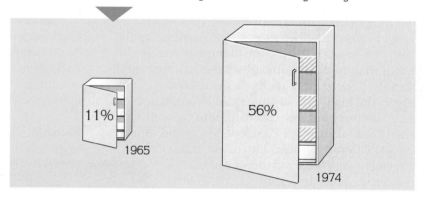

Source E Percentage of Russians owning a refrigerator

11% 1965

56% 1974

Nothing was done to reform the inefficiency of the centrally planned economic system. Source **F** gives an example.

Source F The BBC reporter John Simpson gives an example of Russian economic inefficiency

There is the example of the cement-making plant and the factory which made bags for cement. The two had been built side by side in a small town about 500 miles from Moscow. The central planners required the plastic bags to be sent to Moscow. The cement factory, while it waited for its share of the bags to be sent all the way back, carried on with production in order to fulfil its norm [target]. Often there was nowhere to store the newly-made cement, so it had to be dumped out in the factory yard. The rain quickly turned it into small hills as hard as rock. As far as the managers of the two factories were concerned it was no great problem: their production targets were met and it was someone else's job to get the cement and the plastic bags to the customers.

The War in Afghanistan

Afghanistan was a poor, mountainous country on the southern border of the Soviet Union. In 1979 a group of Muslim freedom fighters, the Mujahidin, were fighting a guerrilla war against the communist Prime Minister Amin. On 27 December the Russian army invaded and replaced Amin with a more moderate communist, Babrak Karmal. The Mujahidin turned their guns on the Russians and Brezhnev's made his greatest mistake.

The Americans had repeatedly warned Brezhnev not to invade. They now helped to arm the Mujahidin.

The Russians were forced to send in more and more troops, but the mountains suited guerrilla fighting and in nine years of war over 13 000 Russian troops were killed and still the Russians could not destroy the Mujahidin.

Détente was destroyed by this war. A second treaty to limit nuclear weapons, SALT II, was abandoned and the Americans stopped supplies of high technology equipment to Russia. America also refused to attend the 1980 Olympic Games in Moscow.

> In 1974 the Ayatollah Khomeini took power. He set up an Islamic republic in Iran, removing all aspects of western life from the country.
> He regarded America as evil. In 1979, 53 Americans in the US Embassy were seized and held hostage for a year.

> The Southern republics of the USSR were mainly Muslim. Their population was increasing quickly, unlike the population of the rest of the USSR. Brezhnev feared that they might become 'infected' with Iran's Muslim, anti-communist political ideas.

SOVIET UNION

IRAN

AFGHANISTAN

PAKISTAN

N

Oil fields on which the West depend

SAUDI ARABIA

0   km   500

Oil to USA, Europe and Japan

> US aid to the mujahidin came through Pakistan. The USA claimed that the Russian army in Afghanistan was a threat to US oil supplies.
> Do you think Russia or Iran was the greater threat to the US?

Source G The War in Afghanistan

The commanding heights?

To many in the West the Soviet Union appeared to be at the height of its power while Brezhnev was in control. On 1 May each year Russia's military power was displayed in Red Square. Its sportsmen and women won huge numbers of gold medals at every Olympic Games. Communism seemed to be making progress around the world. Russian-backed governments took over in the former Portuguese colonies of Angola and Mozambique. The Soviet Union may have lost the race to put a man on the moon, but it could still steal headlines, as in 1971 with its Salyut space station.

However, in reality the Soviet economy could no longer support the expense of being a superpower. The cost of the Space Race, the huge defence budget and the food subsidies were too great.

Source H Russian military might displayed in Red Square

Questions

How successful was Brezhnev?
a) List those policies which you think were a success.
b) Which policy was his greatest success? Give your reasons for this choice.
c) List those policies which were a failure.
d) Which policy was his greatest failure? Give your reasons for this choice.
e) Using the material from your answers to questions **a–d**, answer the question 'How successful was Brezhnev?'

7 The final years of the Soviet Union

Gorbachev and the collapse of the Soviet Union

 **To what extent was the collapse of communist power in the Soviet Union the fault of Gorbachev?
To what extent was it caused by the problems which he inherited?**

After Brezhnev

Brezhnev had wanted his friend and Chief of Staff Konstantin Chernenko to succeed him, even though he was almost as old as Brezhnev himself. In fact the new leader was Yuri Andropov, the former head of the KGB, the Russian secret police – previously known as the NKVD. He wanted to deal with the problems which Brezhnev had ignored, but he soon fell ill and he died after just 18 months as leader. Chernenko then took over, although he himself was now so ill that his deputy, Mikhail Gorbachev, took charge of most Politburo meetings. In 1985 Chernenko died, and Gorbachev became the new General Secretary.

What problems did Gorbachev have to face?

1 The cost of the arms race was too great.
2 The cost of maintaining the communist governments in Eastern Europe was too great.
3 The war in Afghanistan was too expensive and there was no sign of victory.
4 Agriculture was still inefficient and not enough food was being grown.
5 Food subsidies were costing too much.
6 The centrally-planned economic system was unbelievably inefficient.

How successfully did he deal with them?

'Gorbymania'

In the western world Gorbachev quickly became the most popular leader that the Soviet Union had ever produced. At the end of 1987 the US magazine *Time* named him their 'Man of the Year'. He was awarded the Nobel Peace Prize, and when he visited a factory in West Germany in 1989 work stopped as the workers wanted to applaud him. What was it about Gorbachev that made him so popular?

After 40 years of living with the fear of nuclear war, people recognised in Gorbachev a leader who really did want peace between East and West and who wanted to end the Arms Race. Many people may not have realised that Gorbachev had his own motives for wanting these things. He wanted to reform the economy of the Soviet Union, and to do that he needed to end the commitments which the Soviet Union could

Source A US President Reagan and Gorbachev meet as leaders for the first time in 1985. Although this meeting seemed to produce little, it paved the way for the historic INF and CFE treaties.

no longer afford, such as the Arms Race and holding power in Eastern Europe. In 1988 the USA and the Soviet Union signed the INF treaty in which both sides agreed to destroy two categories of nuclear weapons. This was not détente: it was a real move away from nuclear weapons. In 1990 the CFE treaty was signed to limit non-nuclear weapons as well.

The Soviet army also withdrew from Afghanistan, with the final soldier leaving in 1989. A war which had cost 80 billion rubles and the lives of over 13 thousand Russian soldiers had been a total defeat.

'The silence of the telephone'

In August 1989 the Polish trade union Solidarity won 99 out of the 100 senate seats in the first democratic elections to be held in Eastern Europe since the 1940s. The communist President, General Jaruzelski, was asked to comment. 'Sometimes the silence of the telephone is terrifying', he said.

Under the Brezhnev doctrine the states of Eastern Europe had to follow the rules set by the Soviet Union. Failure to do so led to invasion by the Russians, as in Czechoslovakia in 1968. Now things were different. Gorbachev had announced that the Soviet Union would no longer use its military strength to prop up the communist governments of Eastern Europe. Leaders like Jaruzelski would no longer receive telephone calls from Moscow telling them what to do.

The result was that all over Eastern Europe the people demanded free elections. When they took place the communist parties were usually heavily defeated, as Source **B** shows. Only in Romania and Bulgaria did former communists hang on to power, though only after changing to a policy of democratic socialism. The Soviet control of Eastern Europe, which had been maintained with an iron grip since Stalin, collapsed with unbelievable speed.

Source B The Sinatra Doctrine. In the West, Gorbachev's policy of letting the countries of Eastern Europe go their own way was known as the Sinatra Doctrine, after the Frank Sinatra song 'My Way'.

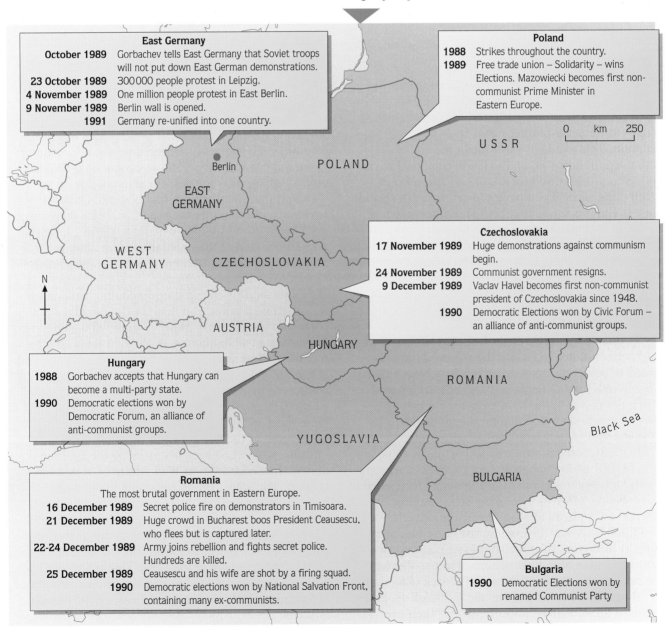

East Germany
October 1989	Gorbachev tells East Germany that Soviet troops will not put down East German demonstrations.
23 October 1989	300 000 people protest in Leipzig.
4 November 1989	One million people protest in East Berlin.
9 November 1989	Berlin wall is opened.
1991	Germany re-unified into one country.

Poland
1988	Strikes throughout the country.
1989	Free trade union – Solidarity – wins Elections. Mazowiecki becomes first non-communist Prime Minister in Eastern Europe.

Czechoslovakia
17 November 1989	Huge demonstrations against communism begin.
24 November 1989	Communist government resigns.
9 December 1989	Vaclav Havel becomes first non-communist president of Czechoslovakia since 1948.
1990	Democratic Elections won by Civic Forum – an alliance of anti-communist groups.

Hungary
1988	Gorbachev accepts that Hungary can become a multi-party state.
1990	Democratic elections won by Democratic Forum, an alliance of anti-communist groups.

Romania
The most brutal government in Eastern Europe.
16 December 1989	Secret police fire on demonstrators in Timisoara.
21 December 1989	Huge crowd in Bucharest boos President Ceausescu, who flees but is captured later.
22-24 December 1989	Army joins rebellion and fights secret police. Hundreds are killed.
25 December 1989	Ceausescu and his wife are shot by a firing squad.
1990	Democratic elections won by National Salvation Front, containing many ex-communists.

Bulgaria
1990	Democratic Elections won by renamed Communist Party

Glasnost and Perestroika

These two Russian words soon became familiar throughout the world. Glasnost means 'openness'. No longer would the Soviet Union be a secretive society. Different opinions could be expressed openly. Dissidents like Andrei Sakharov were released.

Dissidents

Brezhnev had taken a hard line on anyone who openly expressed an opinion which went against the accepted party view. The writer Andrei Solzhenitzyn became the first man since Trotsky to be expelled from the country. Many others were put in psychiatric hospitals. The nuclear physicist Sakharov was exiled to the city of Gorky.

Perestroika was Gorbachev's policy of restructuring the inefficient centrally-planned economy. Many of his supporters, such as the economist Yavlinsky, wanted him to introduce a market – that is, a capitalist economy. This would in effect mean the end of communism in Russia, and so Gorbachev held back. However, he did introduce a Law on Enterprise in 1988. This allowed companies to set most prices and wages. The result was that both shot up, producing inflation. To make matters worse Eastern European countries had provided food for the Soviet Union. With the Sinatra Doctrine, these countries stopped exporting food which was needed to feed their own people. This meant there were food shortages in Russia, so that rationing had to be introduced for the first time since the Second World War.

In order to push through the policy of perestroika, Gorbachev wanted to reduce the power of the party, which he felt prevented enterprise. To achieve this he wanted to return to Lenin's 1924 constitution and give more power to the locally elected soviets. This created great opposition among the nomenklatura, who feared that they would lose their position. Therefore Gorbachev was very unpopular with people who did not want change. In fact Gorbachev was not trying to replace the communist system, but wanted to make it more efficient by making sure that able officials were placed in positions of authority. However, as Source C shows, the Communist Party had little support in Russia. By not abandoning communism, Gorbachev was also making himself unpopular with the people who *did* want change. The lack of food in the shops showed that his way did not work, as people expected an immediate improvement in their lives.

Source C The view of a citizen of Leningrad in April 1990, as reported by BBC correspondent John Simpson

'There's no food, no cars, nothing in the shops. What's the point in having money when there is nothing to buy? I tell you honestly, I've come to hate Gorbachev...I'll tell you something else, I hate the bloody Communists as well. They've wrecked this country, and they don't have the faintest idea how to put things right.'

That view was, I found, entirely representative... No one had a good word to say for the Communist Party or Gorbachev.

The empire strikes back

The Russia which the Bolsheviks took over in 1917 was an empire of 23 different nationalities rather than a country. The Soviet Union became a similar empire. Lenin did not want the USSR to appear as a Russian empire imposed on the non-Russian peoples, in the way that the tsarist empire had been. Education was to take place in the native language. In 1917 there were no schools in the Ukraine which taught in Ukrainian, and 73 per cent of the population were illiterate. By 1927 90 per cent of Ukrainian children were being taught in their native tongue.

However, this changed under Stalin. Nationalism now became a crime and Russian the language of the party and government. Many of those who died in the purges were leading figures in the non-Russian republics. They were replaced by Russians. At the end of the Second World War the Baltic states were conquered by Russia, after a period of independence since 1918. To destroy their desire for nationalism, more than 100 000 of their people were moved to other areas of the Soviet Union especially Siberia. Ukraine, which had been occupied by the Germans during the Second World War, was treated in a similar fashion. The Soviet Union became a Russian empire, and this was resented. Unintentionally, Gorbachev presented them with an opportunity to break free of Russian control. He wanted to reduce the power of the party by giving power to locally elected soviets. In each of the republics of the Soviet Union Supreme Soviets were elected, and in most cases they demanded independence. This was even the case of the Russian Supreme Soviet, which chose Boris Yeltsin as its leader.

Source D 1989: crowds gather under a statue of Lenin in Azerbaijan to demand independence

The Baltic republic of Lithuania simply declared their independence. As Gorbachev had allowed the countries of Eastern Europe their freedom, they believed he should treat the Baltic states in a similar way. However, it was not Gorbachev's policy to allow the Soviet Union to disintegrate. Therefore the MVD – the Russian secret police – were sent in to suppress the rebellion. The sight of Russian tanks on the streets of the Lithuanian capital, Vilnius, destroyed Gorbachev's reputation in the West. Was he really no different to past Russian leaders?

The final blow was not dealt by Lithuania, but by Russia. When the hard line communists failed in their attempt to overthrow Gorbachev in August 1991 (see page 4) the hero was Boris Yeltsin, the recently elected president of Russia. He soon implemented the market reforms which Gorbachev had avoided and the Russian parliament banned the Communist Party. Later that year Gorbachev ceased to be president of a Soviet Union that no longer existed.

Questions

1 Look back to pages 19–20. What evidence can you find that the tsar's minister Stolypin might have agreed with the opinion expressed in Source **E**?

2 Look at pages 60–61. What evidence can you find from Stalin's methods of collectivisation that he might have agreed with Afanassiev?

3 Afanassiev seems to believe that it was not Gorbachev's fault that he failed. It was the fault of the people. Do you agree?
a) Make a list of the failures which you think were Gorbachev's fault.
b) Make a list of the problems he inherited from his predecessors.
c) 'Was Gorbachev to blame for the collapse of the communist system in Russia?' Use examples from your answers to **a** and **b** to support your answer.

Source E By Afanassiev, one of Gorbachev's economic advisers, writing in 1991

Homo sovieticus [Russian man]...is both **ballast** [used to make something stable] and brake. On the one hand, he is opposed to reform, on the other he constitutes the base of support for the existing system.

Yeltsin and 'The End of History'

Source A The state of democracy in Russia. Yeltsin uses tanks to end the opposition of the Russian parliament, 4 October 1993.

The market economy

Having successfully defeated the communists who tried to overthrow Gorbachev in August 1991, Yeltsin was the real hero of Russia. He was the President of the new Russian Federation, and as the Soviet Union collapsed he became the most powerful leader. He set himself two main aims:

1 To abolish the old planned economy and introduce capitalism.
2 To introduce democracy.

He appointed the reformer Yegor Gaidar as prime minister. Gaidar wanted to move to a western style market economy as quickly as possible. In the first year 82 000 state-controlled companies were privatised and by the end of 1993 42 per cent of Russian workers were employed by private firms. On 2 January 1992 Gaidar removed price controls on 90 per cent of goods. The next day prices rose by 250 per cent. Companies could now make a profit and so shops began to fill up with goods, especially imported ones. Many Russian industries could not cope with this foreign competition, and so this produced unemployment. The government became very unpopular.

Under communism the people had got used to having a job and cheap food. The opposition to the reforms was led by the Russian parliament, which had been elected before the fall of communism and so contained many communists. At the end of 1992 Yeltsin tried to win their support by replacing Gaidar with Chernomyrdin, who was known to be less of a reformer. It was not enough. Therefore, in September 1993 Yeltsin decided to dissolve the parliament and hold new elections. He hoped this would produce a parliament which would support him. The parliament refused to accept the decision to hold new elections. Yeltsin chose to defend democracy in a very undemocratic way. Tanks were sent in and they attacked the parliament and forced it to submit.

The new parliament was called the Duma. In fact it did not really support Yeltsin. The largest party in the parliament was Russia's Choice, which was led by Gaidar, and wanted Yeltsin to speed up the pace of reform. The second largest party were the Liberal Democrats, who were extreme nationalists. Led by Vladimir Zhirinovsky they were anti-Semitic and their policies were rather like those of Hitler's. Having slowed down reform Yeltsin was unpopular with Russia's Choice. He was attacked by Zhirinovsky for weakening Russia as a world power.

Chechnya – Yeltsin's Afghanistan?

Although many new countries have been created since the collapse of the Soviet Union, (see Source **C**) this does not mean that the new Russian Federation contains only Russians. In fact there are many different nationalities living in the Federation. The republic of Chechnya lies in the extreme south-west of Russia. It is extremely small and in late 1994 it declared its independence from Russia.

Surprisingly, Yeltsin decided to prevent this by invading Chechnya. Many reformers were horrified. Yeltsin did not consult the parliament. It seemed to prove that Yeltsin had given up reform and was acting like an old-style Russian communist leader. In fact the Russians found it incredibly difficult to defeat the small Chechen army. The war dragged on for months and the Russians suffered heavy casualties. Even after Chechnya had been defeated the Chechens launched a remarkable terrorist attack, capturing a hospital in the Russian town of Budyonnovsk, and holding 1000 patients hostage. The Russian army tried to attack the hospital despite the danger to the hostages, 140 of whom were killed. In the end the terrorists were allowed to leave.

The End of History?

Source B Francis Fukuyama, a US State Department official, writing in 1989

What we may be witnessing is not the end of the Cold War but the end of history as such; that is, the end of man's ideological evolution and the universalisation of Western liberal democracy.

What exactly does Fukuyama mean? He feels that the twentieth century has been a battle between different systems of belief. In the Second World War parliamentary democracy and communism combined to defeat fascism. In the Cold War parliamentary democracy defeated communism. So now only parliamentary democracy is left and he believes that everyone will now accept that this is the best system. Therefore in future all countries will be parliamentary democracies. No longer will history be the story of competing systems of belief.

Source C The End of History? Democracy does not seem to be making progress in the countries that have emerged from the Soviet Union.

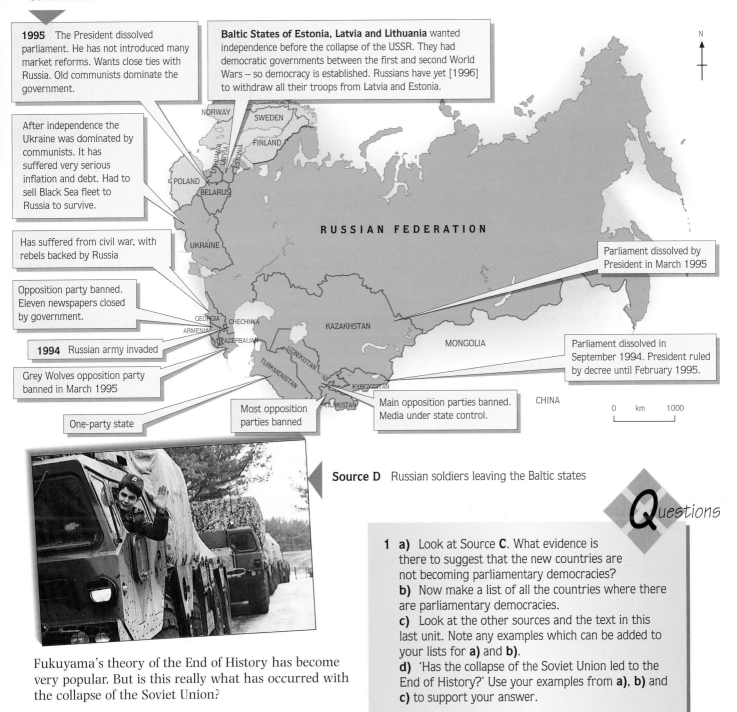

1995 The President dissolved parliament. He has not introduced many market reforms. Wants close ties with Russia. Old communists dominate the government.

Baltic States of Estonia, Latvia and Lithuania wanted independence before the collapse of the USSR. They had democratic governments between the first and second World Wars – so democracy is established. Russians have yet [1996] to withdraw all their troops from Latvia and Estonia.

After independence the Ukraine was dominated by communists. It has suffered very serious inflation and debt. Had to sell Black Sea fleet to Russia to survive.

Has suffered from civil war, with rebels backed by Russia

Opposition party banned. Eleven newspapers closed by government.

1994 Russian army invaded

Grey Wolves opposition party banned in March 1995

One-party state

Most opposition parties banned

Main opposition parties banned. Media under state control.

Parliament dissolved by President in March 1995

Parliament dissolved in September 1994. President ruled by decree until February 1995.

RUSSIAN FEDERATION

NORWAY, SWEDEN, FINLAND, LITHUANIA, LATVIA, ESTONIA, POLAND, BELARUS, UKRAINE, GEORGIA, ARMENIA, AZERBAIJAN, CHECHNYA, TURKMENISTAN, UZBEKISTAN, KAZAKHSTAN, TAJIKISTAN, KYRGYZSTAN, MONGOLIA, CHINA

N

0 km 1000

Source D Russian soldiers leaving the Baltic states

Fukuyama's theory of the End of History has become very popular. But is this really what has occurred with the collapse of the Soviet Union?

Questions

1 a) Look at Source **C**. What evidence is there to suggest that the new countries are not becoming parliamentary democracies?
b) Now make a list of all the countries where there are parliamentary democracies.
c) Look at the other sources and the text in this last unit. Note any examples which can be added to your lists for a) and b).
d) 'Has the collapse of the Soviet Union led to the End of History?' Use your examples from a), b) and c) to support your answer.

Index

Page numbers in **bold** indicate where an explanation or definition is given in a separate panel.